THEMES AND ISSUES

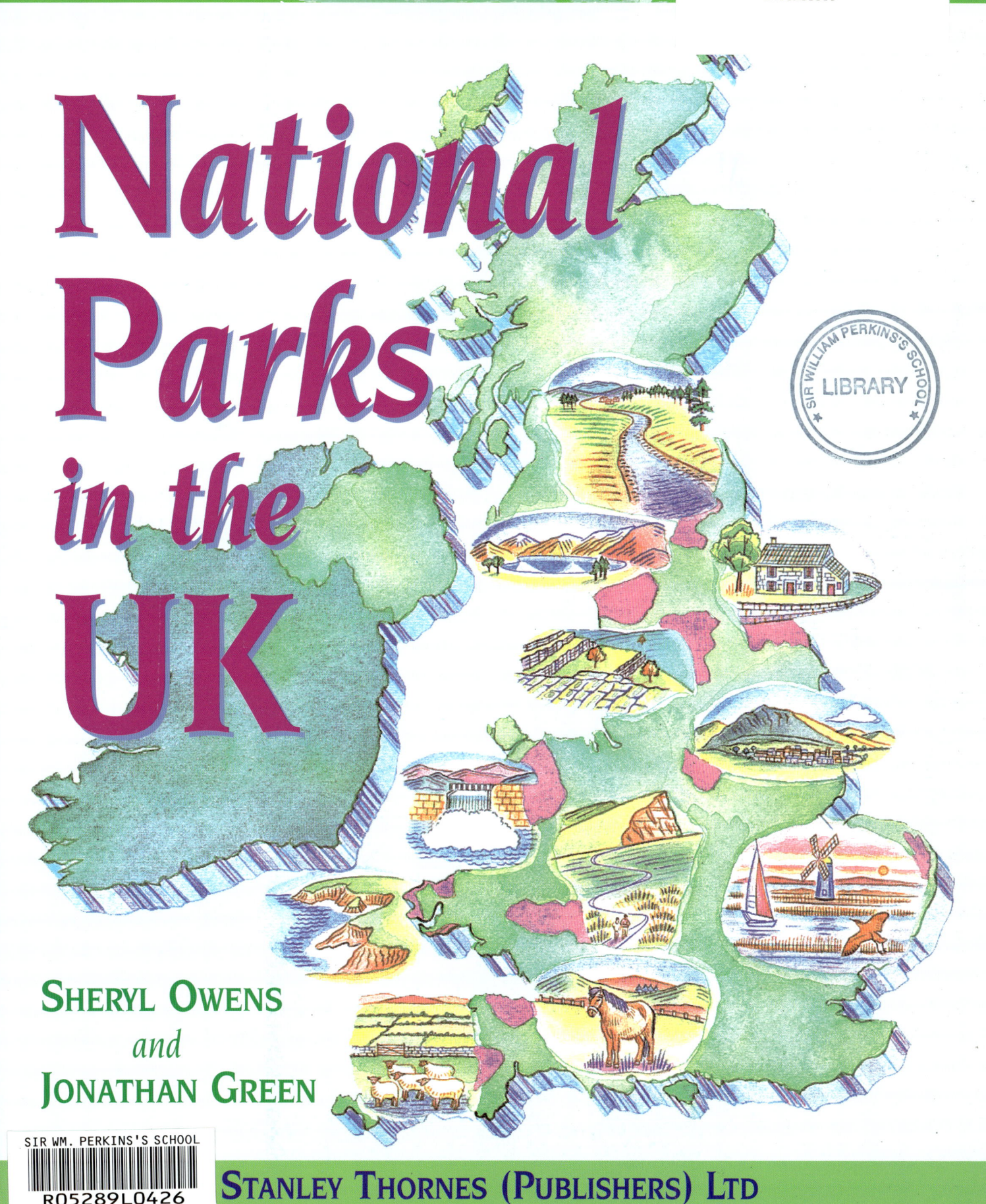

National Parks in the UK

SHERYL OWENS
and
JONATHAN GREEN

STANLEY THORNES (PUBLISHERS) LTD

Text © Sheryl Owens and Jonathan Green 1997

Original line illustrations © Stanley Thornes (Publishers) Ltd 1997

Artwork by Hardlines, David Oliver and Tim Smith

The right of Sheryl Owens and Jonathan Green to be identified as authors of this work has been asserted by them in accordance with the Copyright, Designs and Patents Act 1988.

All rights reserved. No part of this publication may be reproduced or transmitted in any form or by any means, electronic or mechanical, including photocopy, recording or any information storage and retrieval system, without permission in writing from the publisher or under licence from the Copyright Licensing Agency Limited. Further details of such licences (for reprographic reproduction) may be obtained from the Copyright Licensing Agency Limited, of 90 Tottenham Court Road, London W1P 9HE.

First published in 1997 by:
Stanley Thornes (Publishers) Ltd
Ellenborough House
Wellington Street
CHELTENHAM GL50 1YW
England

97 98 99 00 01 / 10 9 8 7 6 5 4 3 2 1

A catalogue record for this book is available from the British Library.

ISBN 0-7487-2879-1

Printed and bound in China

Acknowledgements

The authors and publishers would like to thank the following for permission to reproduce photographs and illustrations in this book:

AA Photolibrary (p. 82 Ja); Rex Features/Huw Evans (pp. 66–7); Science Photo Library/Maptec International (pp. 8–9); Science Photo Library/NRSC Ltd (p. 33); Posy Simmonds (pp. 80–1 I); Terence Soames Photography (pp. 68–9); Jim Soutar (p. 45); Tiv Thomas/Pembrokeshire Coast National Park (p. 18); Windcluster Ltd and PowerGen Renewables Ltd (p. 73); Woodfall Wild Images/David Woodfall (pp. 10, 16); Yorkshire Electricity Group plc (p. 75).

The Ordnance Survey map extracts on pp. 14–15 (Lake District, Landranger 90, 1994), p. 37 (North York Moors, Landranger 94, 1996), p. 40 (Sheffield and Huddersfield, Landranger 110, 1993) and p. 69 (St Davids and Haversfordwest, Landranger 157, 1994) are reproduced from the Ordnance Survey 1:50 000 mapping with the permission of The Controller of Her Majesty's Stationery Office, Crown copyright (07000U).

The authors would like to acknowledge the help of the following:

Brecon Beacons National Park Authority
British Trades Alphabet
Council for National Parks
Countryside Commission
Cumbrian County Council (Corporate Information Unit)
Dartmoor National Park Authority
Duchy of Cornwall Office
Environment Agency
Exmoor National Park Authority
Fairholme Visitor Centre
Forest Enterprise
Forestry Commission
Lake District National Park Authority
Loch Lomond Regional Park
Losehill Hall
Magnox Electric
Mr and Mrs Beaty (Home Farm)

Mr and Mrs Croaker (Runnage Farm)
National Trust
New Forest Committee
Northumberland National Park Authority
North York Moors National Park Authority
Peak National Park Authority
Pembrokeshire Coast National Park Authority
Scottish Council for National Parks
Severn-Trent Water
Snowdonia National Park Authority
Texaco Limited
The Broads Authority
Tilcon Limited
Windcluster Limited
Yorkshire Dales National Park

Every effort has been made to contact copyright holders. The authors and publishers apologise to anyone whose rights have been overlooked, and will be happy to rectify any errors or omissions.

Contents

A map of UK National Parks   4

Introduction   5

1 THE NATIONAL PARKS OF ENGLAND AND WALES   6

2 THE NATURAL LANDSCAPE   10
The role of ice   10
Pembrokeshire and the coast   16
Limestone in the Yorkshire Dales   20
Rivers, water supply and management   24
Woodland and forest management   30

3 THE HUMAN LANDSCAPE   36
Settlement patterns in National Parks   36
Castleton – a honeypot village   38
Accessibility of National Parks   44
The Okehampton bypass – north or south?   46

4 ECONOMIC ACTIVITIES   52
Hill sheep farming   52
Quarrying in the Yorkshire Dales   58
Texaco in Pembrokeshire   64
Energy in the National Parks   70
Tourism – a tertiary industry   76

5 EXMOOR NATIONAL PARK   85

6 PLANNING AND DEVELOPMENT OF THE NATIONAL PARKS   92

Glossary   94

Index   96

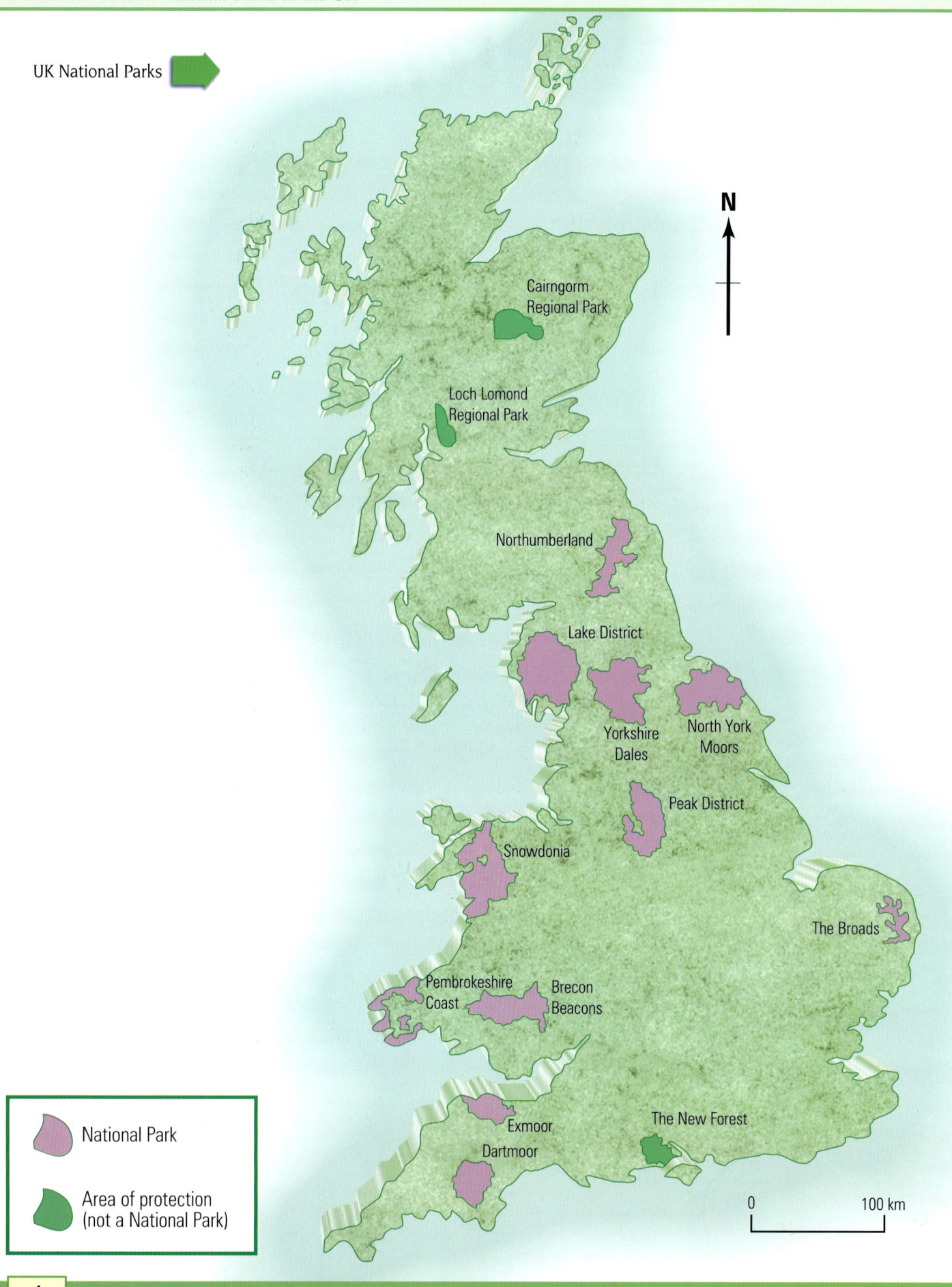

THEMES AND ISSUES: National Parks in the UK

UK National Parks

National Parks shown on the map:
- Cairngorm Regional Park
- Loch Lomond Regional Park
- Northumberland
- Lake District
- Yorkshire Dales
- North York Moors
- Peak District
- Snowdonia
- The Broads
- Pembrokeshire Coast
- Brecon Beacons
- Exmoor
- Dartmoor
- The New Forest

Legend:
- National Park
- Area of protection (not a National Park)

0   100 km

4

Introduction

National Parks in the UK addresses a wide range of geographical ideas and considers the interaction of humans in the natural landscape. The book is designed to be used by GCSE students and to meet many of the requirements of the different syllabuses.

The book looks at case studies from all the National Parks. There are a number of issues which face the parks but it must be stressed that such conflicts are only a minor element in these complex landscapes. By studying a variety of ideas it is hoped that students will develop an awareness of these precious landscapes and the problems that can exist within them.

Within each chapter the book promotes a number of activities which are important to all students studying GCSE Geography. These will provide students with detailed material and practice in essential skills. Five types of activity are included:

- detailed case studies;
- decision making exercises;
- inquiry based skills;
- exam practice questions;
- fieldwork ideas.

Information is given in a variety of ways: in text, photographs and diagrams. Within each chapter there are a number of identifiable features which are designed to be recognisable and make the book easier to use.

- At the start of each section a small map is included to indicate where the case studies are taken from.
- At the start of every section a cross links symbol with page numbers appears in the top right-hand corner to enable students to refer to other areas of the book.
- Certain terms which are in **bold** type in the text are explained in the glossary.
- Bullet points are contained within the text to highlight key ideas and factors.
- Questions are stepped so that all students have access to the information. This also allows for extension work.
- In some sections exam practice questions are given. These are designed to give students experience of questions based on those used by GCSE examining boards. Marks are allocated to these questions.

1 THE NATIONAL PARKS OF ENGLAND AND WALES

National Parks were set up to protect the most beautiful and spectacular areas of countryside in England and Wales. As many people live in crowded towns and cities National Parks also aim to provide opportunities for people to enjoy and appreciate this countryside.

The setting up of National Parks

In 1851 half the population of England and Wales lived in towns and cities. Gradually more and more people wanted to get away from the overcrowded built-up areas. Access to most of the countryside was restricted which led to a public campaign to allow the people the 'right to roam'. In 1932 a major public demonstration took place on Kinder Scout in the Peak District which resulted in many arrests for trespassing.

More people began to press for legislation to allow public access to the countryside. By this time the USA had created the first National Park at Yellowstone. As planning of the countryside became a major issue in the aftermath of the Second World War, the possibility of creating National Parks in the UK was investigated. In 1945 a report was presented to the government by John Dower. He defined a National Park as an extensive area of beautiful and relatively wild countryside in which:

- the characteristic landscape was preserved;
- access and facilities for public open air enjoyment were provided;
- wildlife, buildings and places of historic interest were protected;
- established farming practices were maintained.

These recommendations were debated by the government which resulted in the National Parks and Access to the Countryside Act, 1949. According to this Act, the purpose of National Parks was to:

- preserve and enhance the natural beauty of the area;
- promote the enjoyment of the countryside.

The Act also set up the National Park Commission which later became known as the **Countryside Commission**. Its purpose was to advise the government on which areas should be given National Park status.

Ten areas within England and Wales became National Parks in the 1950s. In 1989 the Broads became the eleventh National Park. The debate over National Parks in Scotland has been an ongoing issue. Whilst Scotland does not have any National Parks, it does have 40 National Scenic Areas as well as Regional Parks at Loch Lomond and the Cairngorms.

Administration of the parks

Each National Park is managed by a **National Park Authority (NPA)**. This is controlled by a committee or board made up of members appointed by the local district and county councils and by the government. The NPA has a number of roles:

- to provide access into the countryside;
- to manage and plant woodland;
- to buy land;
- to develop small-scale projects;
- to advise local landowners;
- to set up and run information centres, car parks and picnic areas;
- to control development.

In 1995 the Environment Act created independent National Park Authorities. This allows the NPAs total control of their area.

Land use and ownership

The National Park Authorities only own a small proportion of the parks. Most of the land is privately owned by farmers, but there are a number of organisations who own land in many of the parks (**A**). Land use within National Parks is varied. On average one-third of the land is open country (moorland, fell, etc.) and one-third is agricultural land (**B**).

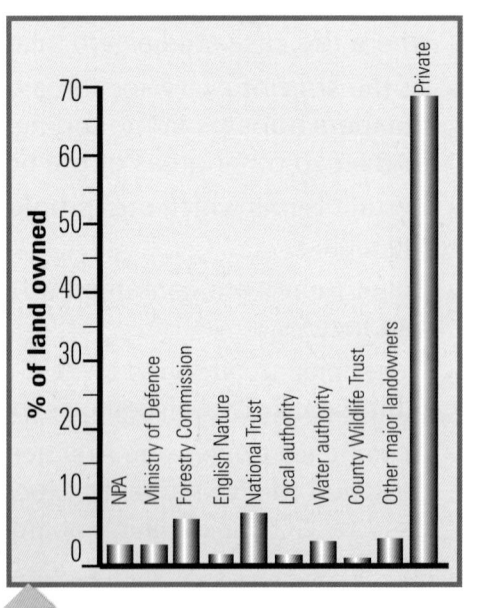

A Land ownership in the National Parks (%)
(Source: Countryside Commission)

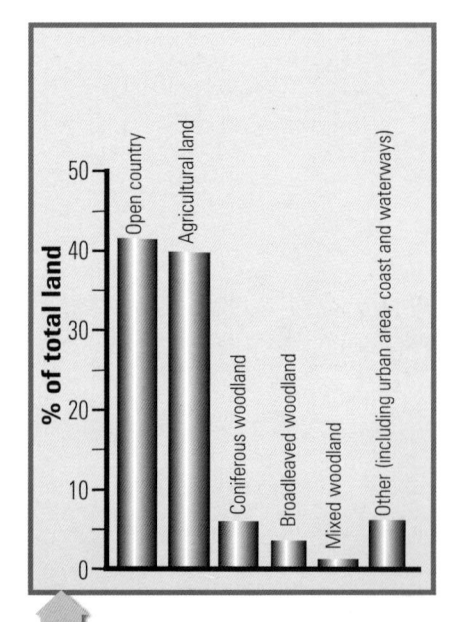

B Land use in the National Parks (%)
(Source: Council for National Parks)

1 The National Parks of England and Wales

Accessibility pp44–5
Tourism pp76–84
Tourism Management p85
Planning and Development pp92–3

C The Lake District National Park

Issues in National Parks

It is very important to remember that National Parks are generally free of problems. They are relatively quiet, unspoilt and unpolluted, especially when compared to other areas of the UK. Problems within National Parks can often be exaggerated when they are studied and this can detract from the beauty and spectacular scenery of these areas (See **D** on pages 8-9).

A major issue affecting all the National Parks is increasing tourism due to more leisure time. This issue can lead to conflicting demands on the landscape:

- People want more access into the countryside.
- There is traffic congestion especially during peak season.
- Visitors want facilities, such as car parks, toilets and picnic areas.
- Local services change to meet the needs of the visitors rather than the local residents.
- More people are buying second homes.
- Problems occur of people walking through farmers' fields.

Other issues can arise that do not involve tourism. For example, the National Park Authority can sometimes discourage new industry from setting up which may have provided jobs for local people.

Activities

1. With the help of an atlas and the map on page 4 describe the distribution of National Parks in England and Wales.
2. Why was there a need for National Parks?
3. Outline the setting up of National Parks.
4. Using **D** on pages 8-9, explain why some National Parks attract more visitors than others.
5. What land uses can you identify in photograph **C**?
6. Study graphs **A** and **B**.
   a. What problem could arise with an increased demand for access into the countryside?
   b. What are the major land uses in National Parks?

7

THEMES AND ISSUES: *National Parks in the UK*

The 11 National Parks of England and Wales **D**

Lake District National Park

Designation year: **1951**   Area (hectares): **229 198**
Population: **42 100**   Visitor days (million per year): **20**

Characteristics and features: This park contains England's highest mountains: Scafell Pike, Helvellyn and Skiddaw. It has 16 large lakes and many glacial landforms such as corries and tarns. The area is mainly moorland and fell. It is popular for walking, climbing and sailing.

Peak National Park

Designation year: **1951**   Area (hectares): **143 833**
Population: **38 100**   Visitor days (million per year): **22**

Characteristics and features: The park is divided into the Dark Peak to the north, made from gritstone, and the White Peak in the south, made from limestone. Kinder Scout is found in the north, whilst the south is characterised by wooded dales, such as Dovedale. The Pennine Way starts at Edale in the centre of the park. Show caves are located around Castleton.

Snowdonia National Park

Designation year: **1951**   Area (hectares): **214 159**
Population: **26 300**   Visitor days (million per year): **11**

Characteristics and features: Mount Snowdon, the largest mountain in England and Wales, is found in this National Park. It also contains much glacial scenery, wide sandy bays, dunes and estuaries. There are many castles in the area and slate mining can still be seen.

Pembrokeshire Coast National Park

Designation year: **1952**   Area (hectares): **58 431**
Population: **23 800**   Visitor days (million per year): **13**

Characteristics and features: This is one of the smallest National Parks. It contains outstanding coastal scenery with rugged cliffs, wide bays and islands. St. David's, Britain's smallest city, is located in the park.

Dartmoor National Park

Designation year: **1951**   Area (hectares): **95 338**
Population: **31 500**   Visitor days (million per year): **8**

Characteristics and features: The area consists of two high granite plateaux divided by the River Dart. It has massive granite tors and steep-sided valleys. Heather covers large areas. Dartmoor has many prehistoric remains as well as England's newest castle which was completed in 1930.

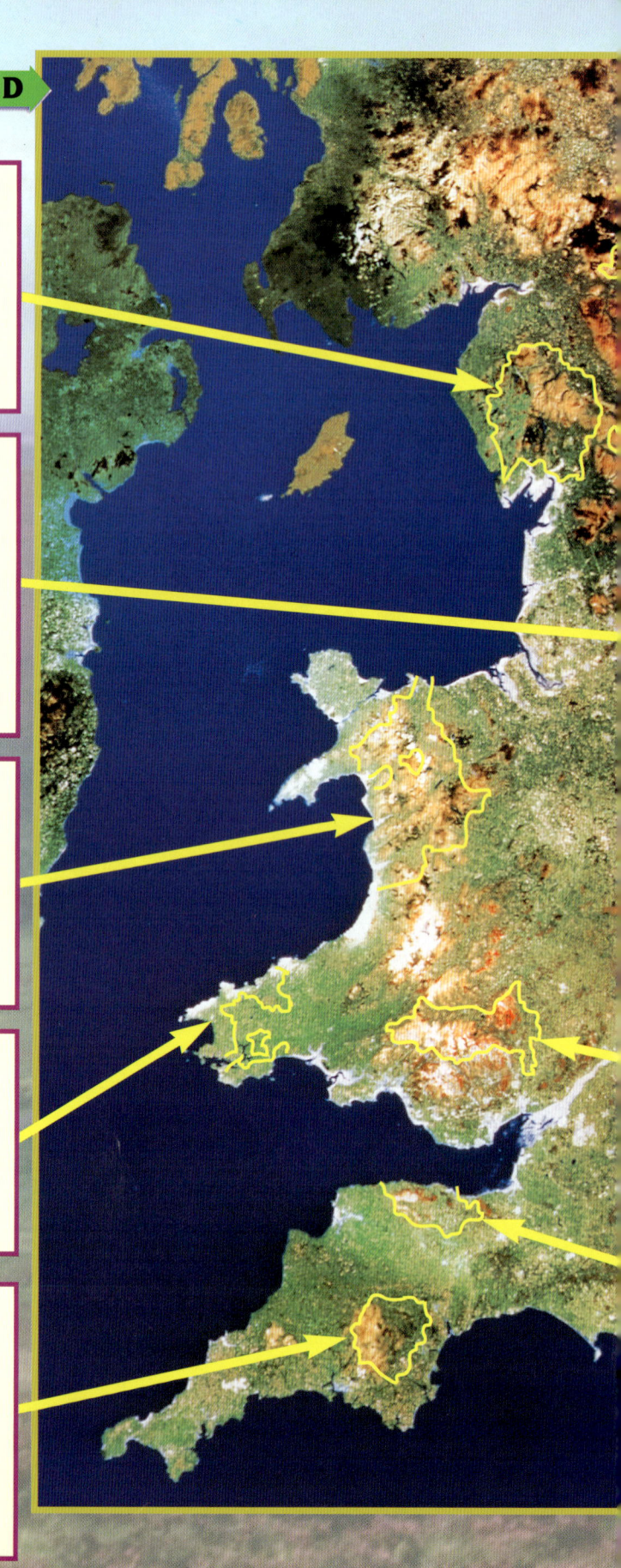

8

1 The National Parks of England and Wales

Northumberland National Park

Designation year: **1956**   Area (hectares): **104 947**
Population: **2200**   Visitor days (million per year): **1**

Characteristics and features: This is one of the remotest parks and contains mainly moorland. The north west border is on the boundary of England and Scotland and has sections of Hadrian's Wall. Part of the Pennine Way runs the length of the park.

North York Moors National Park

Designation year: **1952**   Area (hectares): **143 603**
Population: **25 000**   Visitor days (million per year): **11**

Characteristics and features: This has moorland and a rugged Heritage coastline with high cliffs and wide bays. The Cleveland Way is a long-distance footpath which passes through many picturesque fishing villages, such as Staithes.

Yorkshire Dales National Park

Designation year: **1954**   Area (hectares): **176 869**
Population: **19 100**   Visitor days (million per year): **9**

Characteristics and features: This upland area consists of moorland and broad pastoral valleys. The three main peaks of Ingleborough, Pen-y-Gent and Whernside are made of gritstone. Scars and pavements can be seen in the landscape where limestone is exposed. There are several long-distance footpaths including part of the Pennine Way, Dales Way and Ribble Way.

The Broads

Designation year: **1989**   Area (hectares): **30 292**
Population: **5500**   Visitor days (million per year): **3**

Characteristics and features: The area contains 25 broads which were made by humans. They are the flooded remains of peat pits which were dug in mediaeval times. The area also has fens, slow winding waterways and marshland. It has spectacular wildlife including rare species of birds and insects. It has 201 kilometres of navigable water.

Brecon Beacons National Park

Designation year: **1957**   Area (hectares): **135 144**
Population: **32 200**   Visitor days (million per year): **7**

Characteristics and features: This region has sandstone moors and areas of millstone grit and limestone. It contains Britain's longest known cave system and has the only canal in any of the National Parks. Pen-y-fan is the highest mountain in the Beacons whilst to the east the Black Mountains stretch to the English border.

Exmoor National Park

Designation year: **1954**   Area (hectares): **68 637**
Population: **10 000**   Visitor days (million per year): **3**

Characteristics and features: The area has a wide variety of landscapes from a dramatic coastline to heather moors and wooded combes. It contains an ancient wooded forest and has wild red deer and ponies.

2 THE NATURAL LANDSCAPE

National Parks are areas of outstanding natural scenery. These landscapes have been sculptured by a variety of natural and human processes over thousands of years. Each park has its own characteristic landscape as a result of the interrelationships between these processes.

The role of ice

The last major Ice Age in Britain began about 2 million years ago and ended 10 000 years ago. The work of the ice and the dramatic landforms it created can still be seen in the National Parks. **Glaciation** is the term used where ice is active in the landscape eroding, transporting and depositing material. Today the UK has no permanent ice. Glaciation continues in areas of high altitude in other parts of the world, such as the Alps, the Himalayas and in the polar regions (**B**).

B Ice in a present day glaciated area

Cwm Idwal and Nant Ffrancon

The Cwm Idwal and Nant Ffrancon area lies to the north of the Snowdonia National Park and is one of the most spectacular glaciated landscapes in the UK. Many glacial features formed by erosion and deposition can be seen in this upland area.

The formation of Cwm Idwal

- At the start of the last glaciation when the climate cooled, a north facing hollow on the side of the Glyder mountain range began to collect snow. This became compressed and turned to ice.
- Over hundreds of years freeze-thaw (**A**) enlarged the hollow and allowed further accumulation of snow and ice. As this patch of ice grew, a corrie glacier developed which shaped the land by the processes of freeze-thaw, abrasion and plucking (**D**). Abrasion occurs when the ice contains fragments of rock which act like sandpaper to wear away the ground. Plucking is when ice freezes to rock on the valley floor or sides. As the ice moves, parts of the rock are pulled away.
- In the area where two corries eroded next to each other a knife-edged ridge formed. This is known as an arête.

A Freeze-thaw weathering

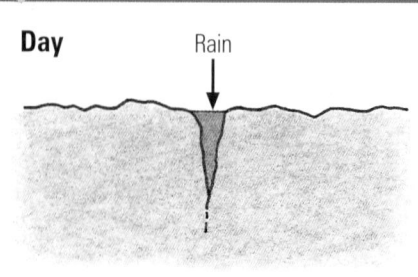

Day — Rain

The surface of the land is uneven with many small cracks. Water may collect in these cracks.

Night — Water freezes

As the temperature falls below zero degrees Celsius at night the water freezes and expands. This puts pressure on the sides of the crack.

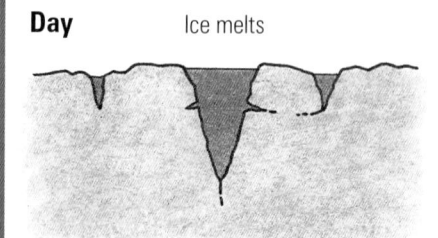

Day — Ice melts

As the temperature increases in the day the ice melts and the pressure is released.

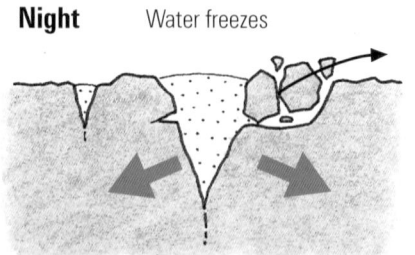

Night — Water freezes

This process of freeze-thaw (or frost shattering) continues and enlarges the crack. Fragments of rock are levered apart and may fall or be washed away.

2 The Natural Landscape

River Breamish pp24–5
Farming p52
Tourism pp76–81
Footpath erosion pp82–3

- The rock fragments became incorporated into the ice and moved along with it to be deposited when the ice melted.
- At the end of the Ice Age as the temperature increased the ice melted to leave behind the basin shaped landform known as a corrie (cirque or cwm). Many corries have a deep rounded lake known as a tarn. The water is contained within the hollow and is often dammed by the rock lip or moraine (**C** and **D**).

Cwm Idwal and its lake **C**

D Processes in the formation of a corrie glacier

1 The rotatory movement of the ice produces a deep basin-like shape.

2 Freeze-thaw and plucking create the characteristic steep back wall.

3 A large crevasse, known as a bergschrund, is found at the back of the corrie which allows material to fall into the glacier.

4 At the base of the glacier material is ground down by abrasion to form a **rock flour**.

5 Abrasion deepens the hollow.

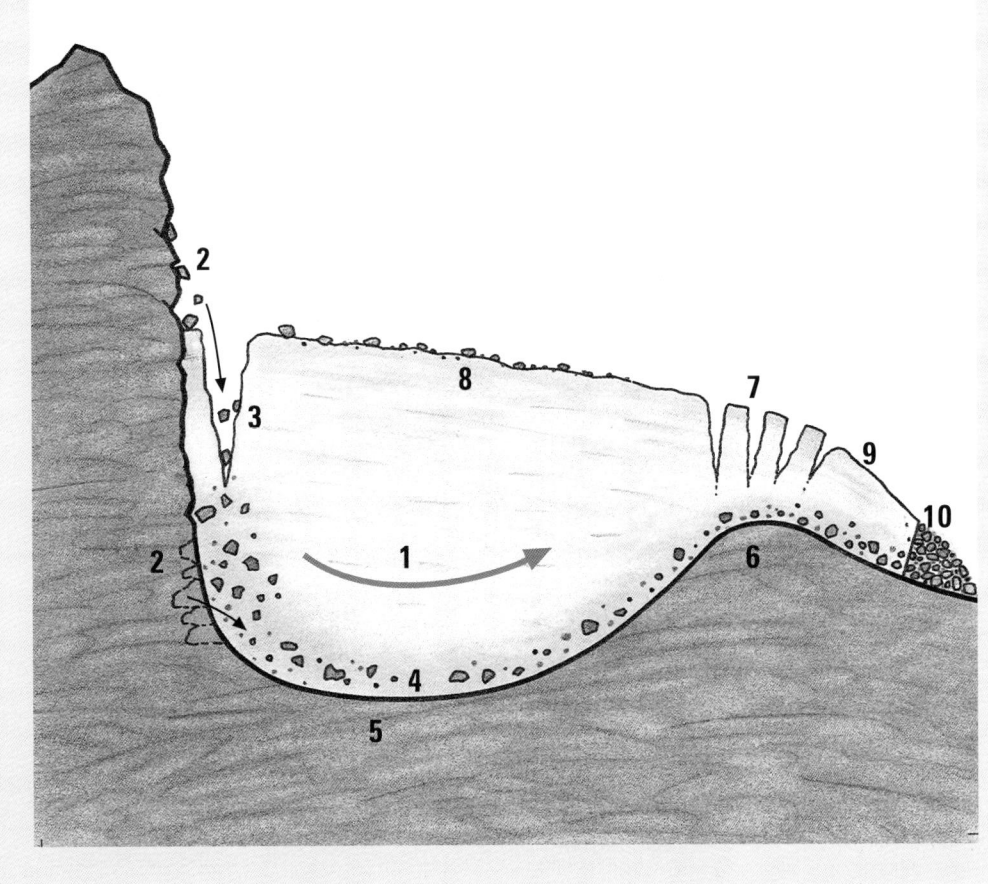

6 The corrie glacier is dammed by a rock lip where erosion is not so great.

7 As the ice passes over the rock lip an ice fall is produced which consists of crevasses and seracs (upright pieces of ice).

8 Fresh layers of snow may be added.

9 If the ice passes over the rock lip and moves downhill it becomes a valley glacier.

10 Melting at the glacier snout causes rock debris to be deposited. This is called moraine.

THEMES AND ISSUES: National Parks in the UK

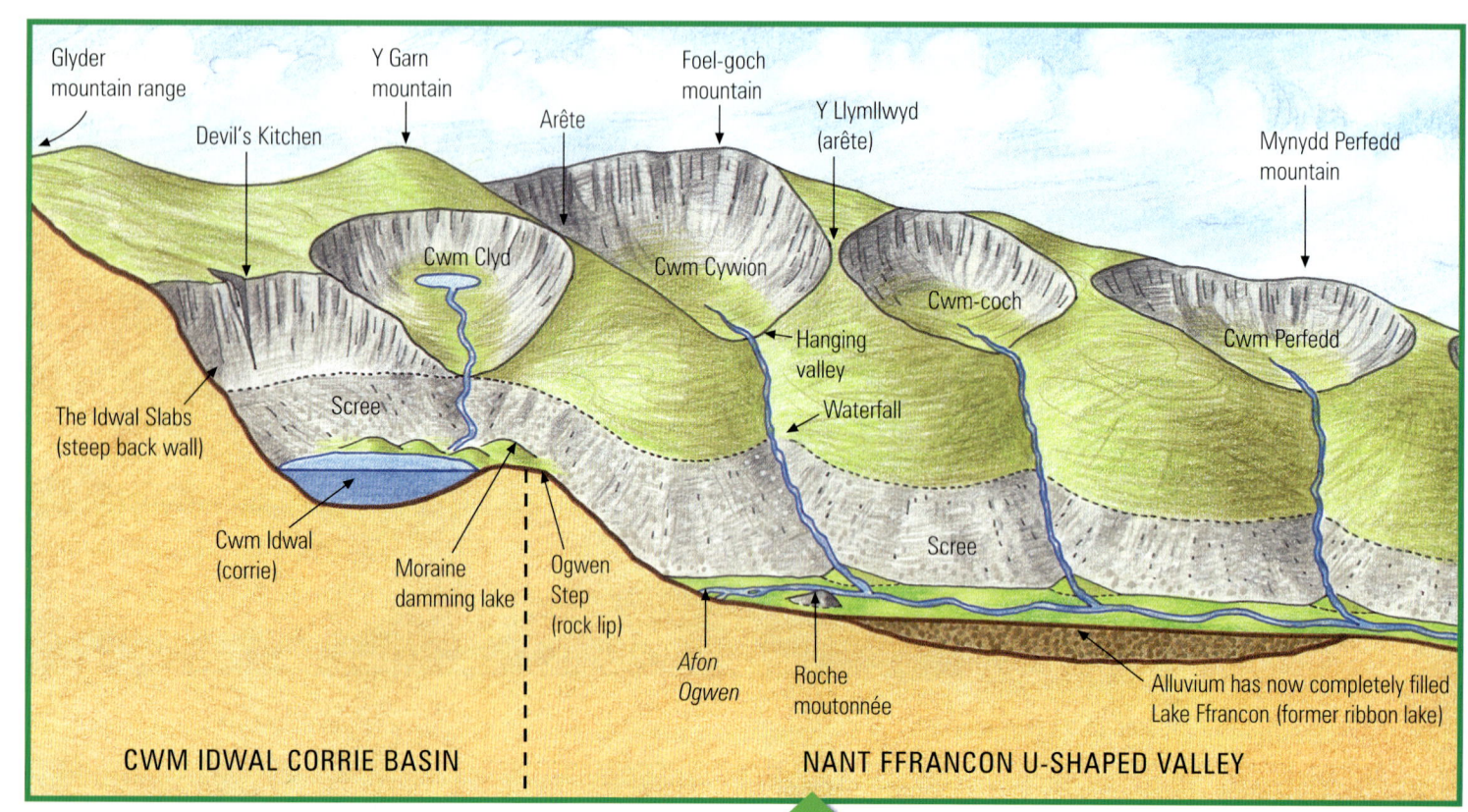

E Cross section of the Cwm Idwal and Nant Ffrancon area

The formation of the Nant Ffrancon valley

As the corrie glaciers in the area grew and expanded downhill, they joined to form a valley glacier. This ice followed the existing river course of the Afon Ogwen. The powerful glacier straightened the river valley creating **truncated spurs**. The valley was eroded by the material carried in the ice to create a U-shaped valley. This is characterised by steep sides and a flat valley floor.

This feature has been modified since the ice in the area melted. Glacial processes no longer operate apart from freeze-thaw in the high mountain area. Where material is generated it falls and collects along the valley sides as scree slopes. Afon Ogwen (**E**) still runs through the Nant Ffrancon valley but as it did not create the wide flat floor, it is known as a **misfit** (**F**).

Cwm Cywion was formed by a smaller corrie glacier which fed the valley glacier occupying the Nant Ffrancon. As there was less ice in this feeder glacier,

F Looking down Nant Ffrancon

it was not as powerful and did not erode to the same level as the Nant Ffrancon valley. When the ice melted, the corrie and valley were left perched above the main valley floor. This is known as a hanging valley and often contains a waterfall.

A ribbon lake is an elongated body of water found in the bottom of U-shaped valleys. The remains of a ribbon lake can be found in the Nant Ffrancon valley but it has long since become silted up by alluvium. This is material deposited by the river. Today this forms good fertile farmland (**F**). A ribbon lake is formed by the over deepening of the valley floor and is often dammed by moraine. This occurs when either:

- the glacier becomes more powerful due to increased ice; or
- the glacier passes over a band of less resistant rock.

The Nant Ffrancon valley has one of the best examples of a roche moutonnée in the UK (**G**). This was formed as ice passed over a resistant piece of rock eroding the surrounding area. Abrasion smoothed the leading side of the rock whilst plucking created a jagged downhill side. The leading side is marked by striations which form when ice and rocks scratch the surface.

Types of moraine in Cwm Idwal and Nant Ffrancon

- **Terminal moraine** - this was deposited at the snout of the glacier when the ice melted.
- **Ground moraine** - as the glacier moved downhill, rock debris and flour was deposited along the valley floor.
- **Lateral moraine** - material was carried at the sides of the ice. When the ice melted, this material was deposited along the sides of the valley.
- **Medial moraine** - when feeder glaciers joined the Nant Ffrancon the lateral moraines were pushed towards the middle of the valley glacier.

People in the glaciated landscape

In most glaciated areas sheep farming is the main economic activity. The thin acidic soils on the valley sides and the climatic conditions in these upland areas often make this the only profitable land use. However, the more fertile valley floors can be put to other uses.

The glacial scenery offers many opportunities for sporting activities. For example, in the Cwm Idwal and Nant Ffrancon area the Idwal Slabs are used for climbing and the numerous footpaths encourage walking and cycling. The increased number of people taking part in these outdoor activities has led to the growth of climbing and rambling shops in nearby villages (for example Betws-y-coed). In other National Parks ribbon lakes provide excellent opportunities for water sports and leisure cruises (for example Windermere). With this increasing demand on glaciated landscapes problems such as footpath erosion sometimes occur.

G A roche moutonnée in the Nant Ffrancon valley

THEMES AND ISSUES: National Parks in the UK

Glaciation in the Lake District

The Lake District is an area of dramatic glaciated scenery from the jagged mountain tops and fells to the U-shaped valley floors and elongated ribbon lakes. The centre of the Lake District was covered with an ice sheet from which valley glaciers eroded downwards and outwards. Evidence of corrie glaciers can also be found in the landscape. This pattern of erosion can still be seen. Today the landscape offers great scope for leisure activities and so attracts a large number of visitors.

H OS map extract from the Lake D

I

J

Exam practice

1 Match the photographs (**I, J, K** and **L**) to their appropriate feature. Choose from the following list: hanging valley, U-shaped valley, moraine and tarn. Give a six-figure grid reference using the OS map extract (**H**) for each of these features. *(4 marks)*

2 Great Langdale is a valley in the Lake District. Use the photographs and map to:

   a describe its appearance;

   b explain its formation. *(6 marks)*

14

2 The Natural Landscape

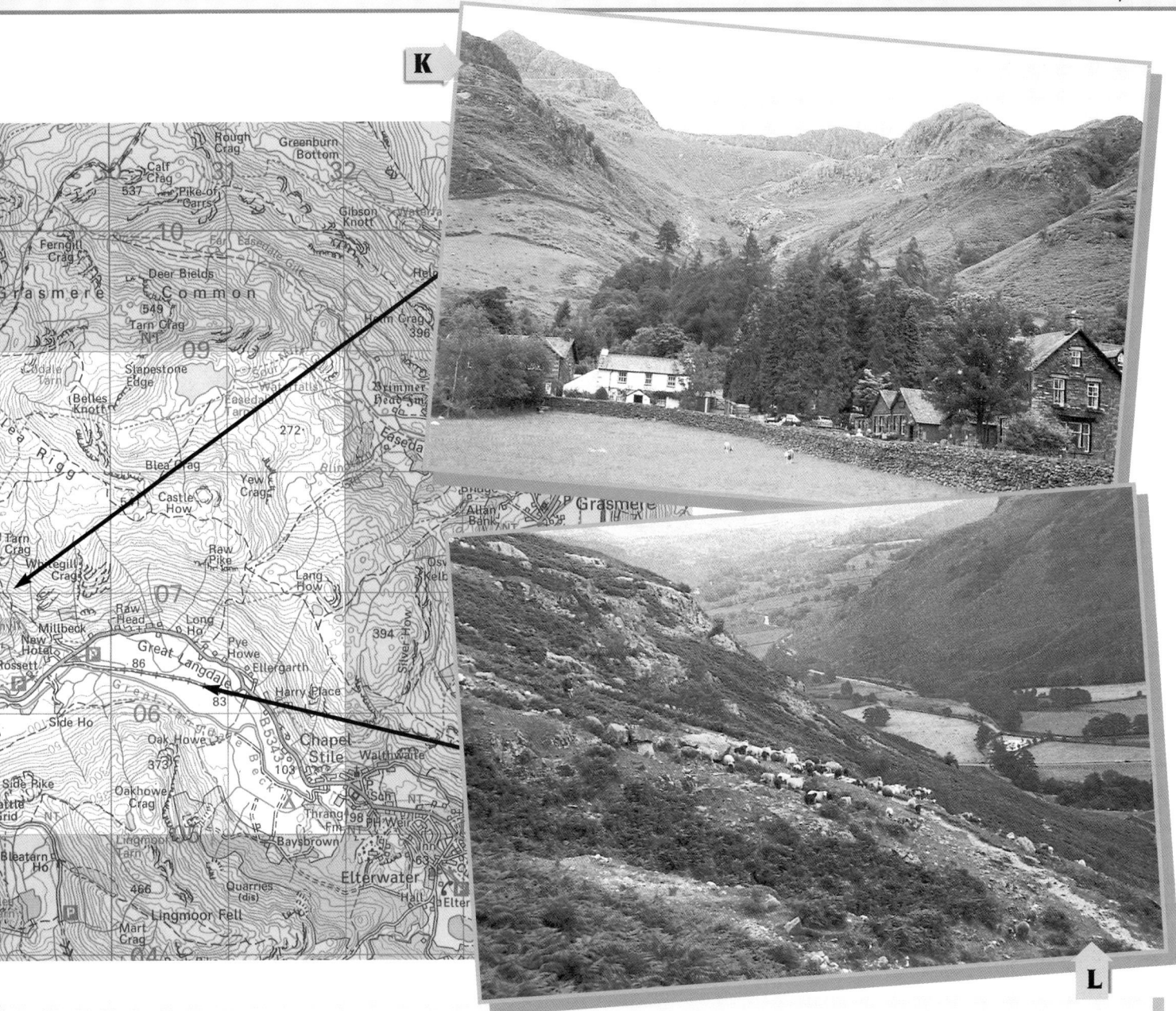

3 What direction did the ice move along Great Langdale. Give a reason for your choice of direction.
(2 marks)

4 Study photograph **L** and the OS map extract.
  a Give three land uses of the valley floor in Great Langdale.
  b Give two land uses of the valley sides.
  c Explain this pattern of land use.
(8 marks)

5 a What are the four types of moraine and how are they formed?
  b What type of moraine might you expect to find at the end of a glacial lake? (6 marks)

6 a List four physical characteristics of the corrie found in grid square 3008.
  b Explain as fully as possible how this corrie was created. Illustrate your answer with sketches. (8 marks)

7 How is a hanging valley formed?
(3 marks)

8 What recreational activity would be suitable at the following locations:
  a 298072;   **b** 280074;
  c 300063. (3 marks)

9 The physical landscape provides many opportunities for recreation. Explain how the area shown in the map could be used for leisure activities. (6 marks)

Pembrokeshire and th

Pembrokeshire is the only predominantly coastal National Park in England and Wales. This area of outstanding natural beauty contains important areas for conservation. It has a rich cultural heritage and a great variety of geographical landforms. Pembrokeshire is visited by over 13 million people a year, who go to the beaches, take part in water sports, walking or climbing.

Pembrokeshire consists of bands of different rock which have been gradually moulded by coastal processes and the action of glacial meltwater. The area has two main headlands of resistant rock, St. David's Head and St. Ann's Head, between which is St. Brides Bay composed of softer rock. Along the coastline there are many smaller headlands and bays (**A**).

The Pembrokeshire Coast National Park **A**

The landforms can be divided into three categories according to the processes that formed them:
- erosional (for example cliffs, wave cut platforms, caves, etc.);
- depositional (for example beaches, dunes, mudflats, salt marshes);
- changes in sea level (for example raised beaches and rias).

The Green Bridge of Wales **B**

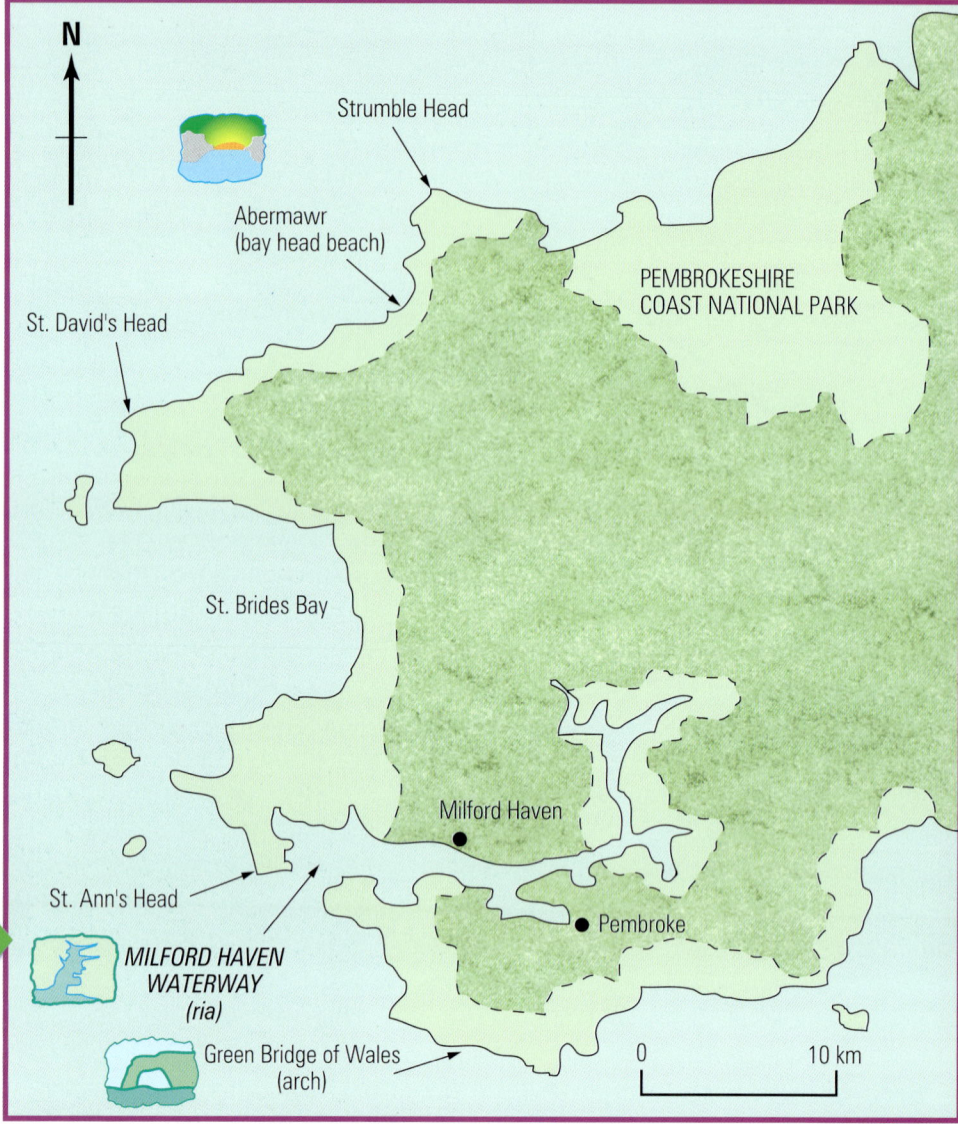

2 The Natural Landscape

National Park pp7–8
Milford Haven Waterway pp64–9
Tourism pp76–84
Planning and development pp92–3

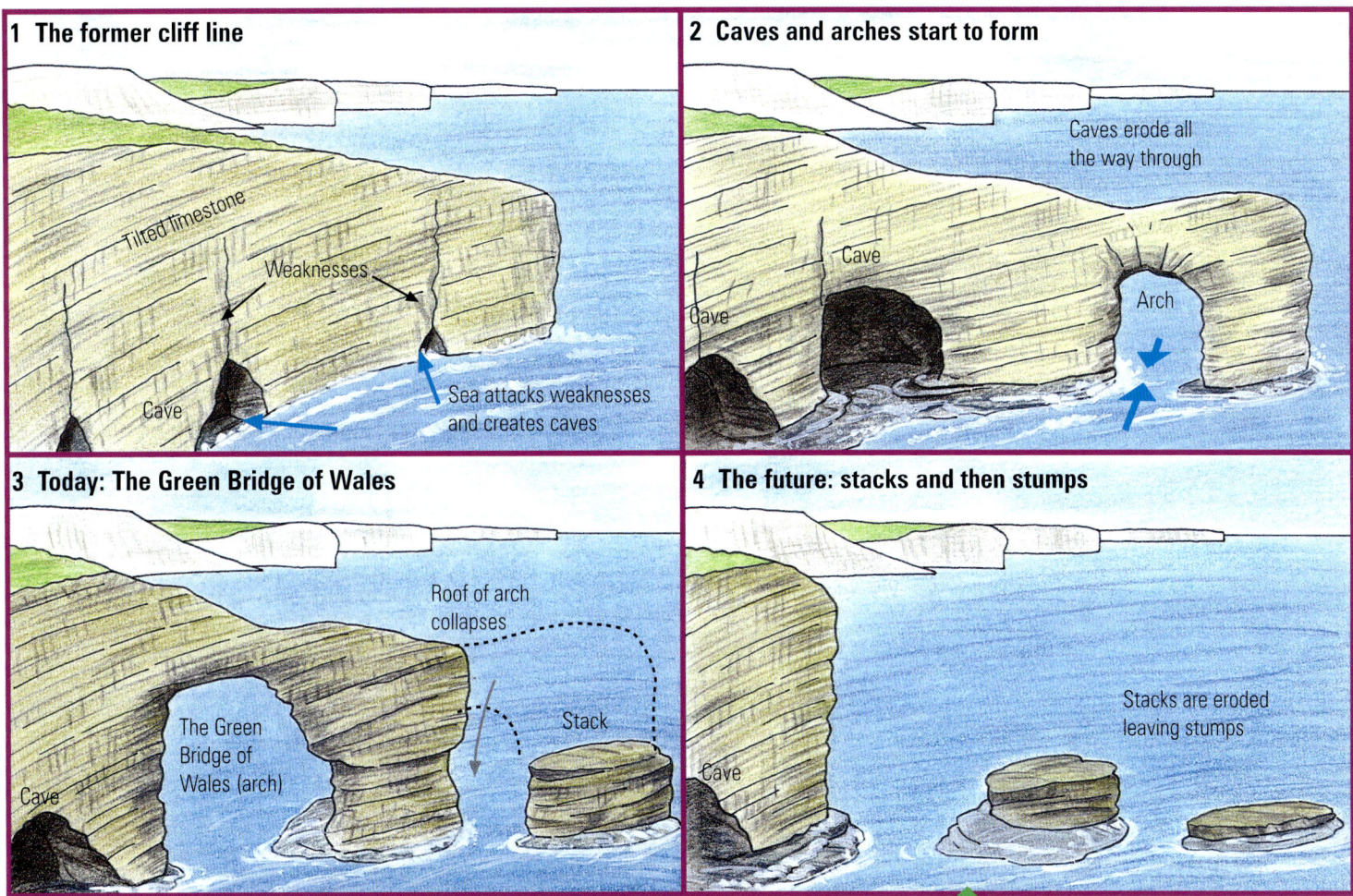

coast

1 The former cliff line
- Tilted limestone
- Weaknesses
- Cave
- Sea attacks weaknesses and creates caves

2 Caves and arches start to form
- Caves erode all the way through
- Cave
- Cave
- Arch

3 Today: The Green Bridge of Wales
- Roof of arch collapses
- The Green Bridge of Wales (arch)
- Cave
- Stack

4 The future: stacks and then stumps
- Cave
- Stacks are eroded leaving stumps

C The formation of the Green Bridge of Wales

The Green Bridge of Wales – an erosional feature

The Green Bridge of Wales is a sea arch located on the Castlemartin peninsula. It is made from carboniferous limestone, which has a well jointed structure and is tilted at an angle (**B**). It is the greenish tinge of the rock that gave the arch its name.

The Pembrokeshire coastline is attacked by waves from the south west. The waves are formed over a distance of approximately 7000 kilometres. This is known as the fetch; the longer the distance the more powerful the waves can become. On average the cliffs experience between 25 and 30 days of gale force winds a year. These waves erode the base of the cliff by two main processes:

- hydraulic action – the waves crash against the rock trapping air in the cracks. As this is repeated the rock begins to weaken under the pressure and fragments will fall away.

- abrasion – the fragments of rock carried by the waves are thrown against the cliff. This chips away the base of the cliff.

The sea attacks weaknesses in the rock by abrasion and hydraulic action. This continues for many years until a cave is formed. The cave is enlarged by the sea and the weather. When two caves join an arch is formed. The erosion continues until the roof of the arch is no longer supported and it collapses into the sea. The remnant is called a stack. The stack is eroded downwards to leave a stump (**C**).

Activities

1. How do waves alter the coastline?
2. What is the fetch?
3. Study photograph **B** and describe the structure of the rock.
4. Explain, with the aid of a diagram, how an arch might be formed.

17

THEMES AND ISSUES: **National Parks in the UK**

D The action of waves

E Bay head beach at Abermawr

F The formation of a ria

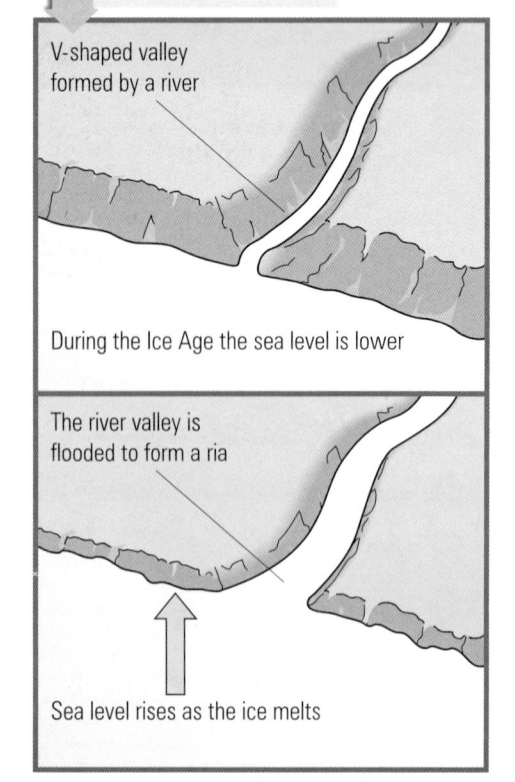

V-shaped valley formed by a river

During the Ice Age the sea level is lower

The river valley is flooded to form a ria

Sea level rises as the ice melts

Abermawr beach – a depositional feature

Over 90 per cent of all depositional features are beaches. The most common type of beach in Pembrokeshire is the bay head beach, between two headlands. A small-scale example is Abermawr beach. This beach is about half a kilometre in length and is composed of materials of varying sizes, the majority of which are pebbles.

It has been produced by the erosion of hard and soft rock. Wave energy is concentrated on the headlands at either side of the beach. Here the rock is more resistant but particles are eroded from them and then deposited in the bay. Material is also deposited in the bay from along the coastline by **longshore drift** (**D**), from the river entering the bay and from offshore.

The wave action sorts out material on the beach (**D**). The waves break carrying material up the beach. This is known as the swash. The heaviest material is deposited at the top of the beach whilst the lighter material is dragged back towards the sea. This is known as the backwash. Therefore the sand is found by the shoreline, whilst the pebbles are banked up towards the rear of the beach. During high tides and storm conditions the large material is deposited high up the beach forming a ridge. This is known as a storm beach (**E**).

Milford Haven – a ria

One of the best examples in the UK of a ria, also known as a drowned river valley, is the Milford Haven Waterway. During the Ice Age the sea level was much lower than it is today. Normal river processes were at work and cut into the landscape, producing a wide river valley before entering the sea. When the ice melted and the sea level rose by about 30 metres, the lower sections of the river valley and adjacent river valleys were flooded (**F**).

Today the ria extends about 20 kilometres inland. It contains mud flat and sand dune systems and is an important area for wildlife. The ria also provides a deep water port for oil tankers and the oil refining industry at the town of Milford Haven.

2 The Natural Landscape

Management and the Pembrokeshire coast

Pembrokeshire is managed by the National Park Authority which is responsible for the overall planning of the area. National Park rangers work in the area supervising conservation projects. They also organise walks, talks and activities in the Pembrokeshire Coast National Park.

Pembrokeshire has 13 sand dune systems which support a rich variety of flora. Many areas have suffered from the pressure of recreational use. Damage was caused to dunes at Freshwater East by people taking short cuts to the beach, playing football, sledging and using motorbikes and four-wheel drives. The dune system nearly vanished and had to be rebuilt using a JCB. Extensive marram grass planting was undertaken by members of the public. Information boards were used to explain the work being carried out and visitors were channelled to the beach from the car park by well defined paths.

Erosion is a natural process along the Pembrokeshire coastline but intervention is occasionally necessary. For example, Amroth is a village that is threatened by the sea during storm conditions. Sea defences have now been built to protect the village. At Tenby beach attempts have been made to stabilise the movement of sand. **Groynes** have been built at regular intervals along the beach which trap the sand.

In some places where cliffs have collapsed the Pembrokeshire Coast path is affected. A new right of way needs to be created by negotiations between the National Park Authority and the land-owner. The National Park Authority actually has the power of compulsory purchase but would only use this as a last resort and would rather sort out a problem amicably.

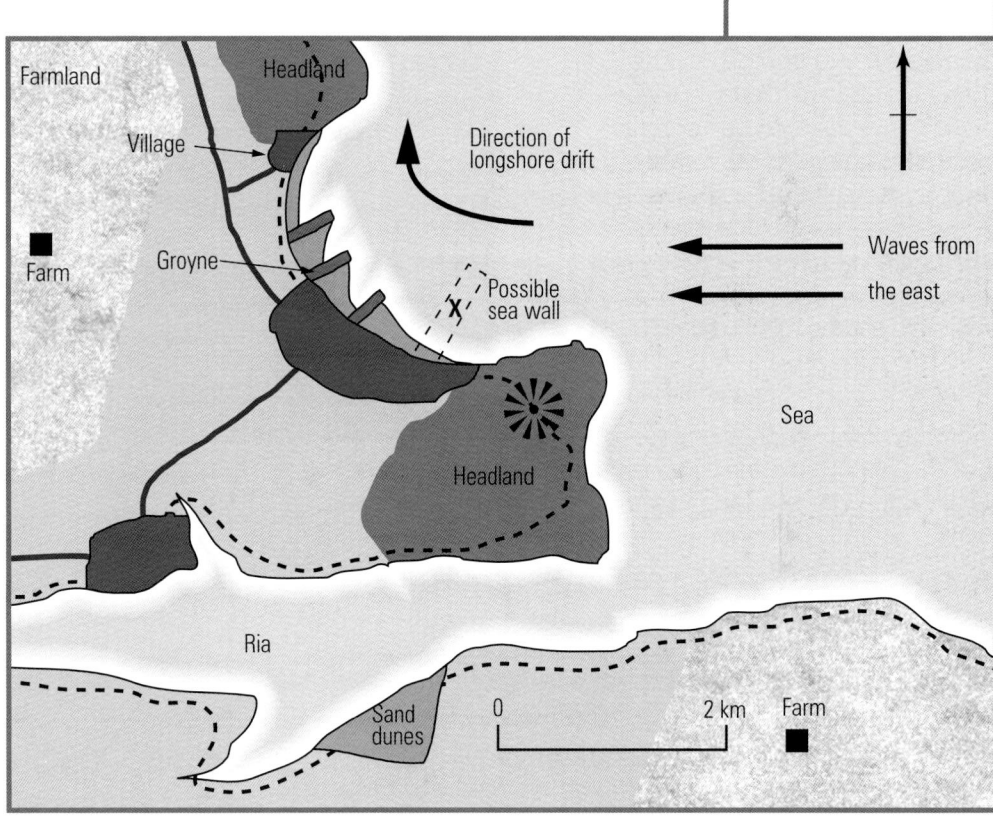

G

Key
- Town
- Farmland
- Higher ground
- Beach
- Road
- Coastal path
- Viewpoint
- Groyne

Exam practice

Using diagram **G** answer the following questions:

1 Draw an outline sketch of **G** and label an area of:
 • more resistant rock;
 • less resistant rock;
 • erosion;
 • deposition. *(4 marks)*

2 What is a groyne? Explain how it works. *(2 marks)*

3 What effect would the building of a new sea wall at **X** have on the coastline? *(3 marks)*

4 What value would a ria offer to human activity? *(4 marks)*

5 State two attractions for tourists in this area. *(2 marks)*

6 Discuss one conflict that might arise due to tourists in the area. *(4 marks)*

7 Explain how human activity may affect the natural processes and beauty along this coastline. *(6 marks)*

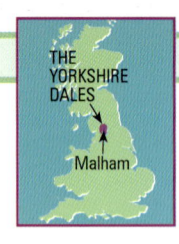

Limestone in the Yorkshire Dales

Carboniferous limestone forms a dramatic upland landscape which can be seen in a number of National Parks. The Yorkshire Dales contain large areas of the rock and have some of the best examples of limestone features.

A Services in Malham

Carboniferous limestone is a hard, grey rock that formed about 350 million years ago when sea creatures collected and fossilised on the sea floor. The rock was compressed into layers with a high content of calcium carbonate. These layers were separated by horizontal **bedding planes**. As the rock dried, vertical cracks, known as **joints**, formed to give limestone its characteristic structure. Limestone is pervious, which means that water is allowed to pass along the joints and bedding planes. The rock itself is impermeable as it is solid.

Limestone is weathered by a process known as carbonation. Rainwater acts as a weak carbonic acid which converts the calcium carbonate in the limestone into calcium bicarbonate. This is soluble and can be washed away by water.

$$CaCO_3 + H_2O + CO_2 = Ca(HCO_3)_2$$

Calcium carbonate + water + carbon dioxide = calcium bicarbonate

Carbonation is responsible for many of the features found around Malham in the Yorkshire Dales (**B**). This landscape attracts over a million people each year who come to visit the spectacular scenery.

Limestone landscape around Malham

① Malham village

Malham lies eight kilometres east of Settle in the Yorkshire Dales. The roads in the area have not been upgraded for the amount of traffic that uses them. Despite this, Malham has become a successful **honeypot** site. The village has a population of approximately 400. However, the majority of services offered cater for the visitors. The village has a visitor centre, numerous cafés, shops, bed and breakfast accommodation and hotels (**A**).

B Limestone features around Malham

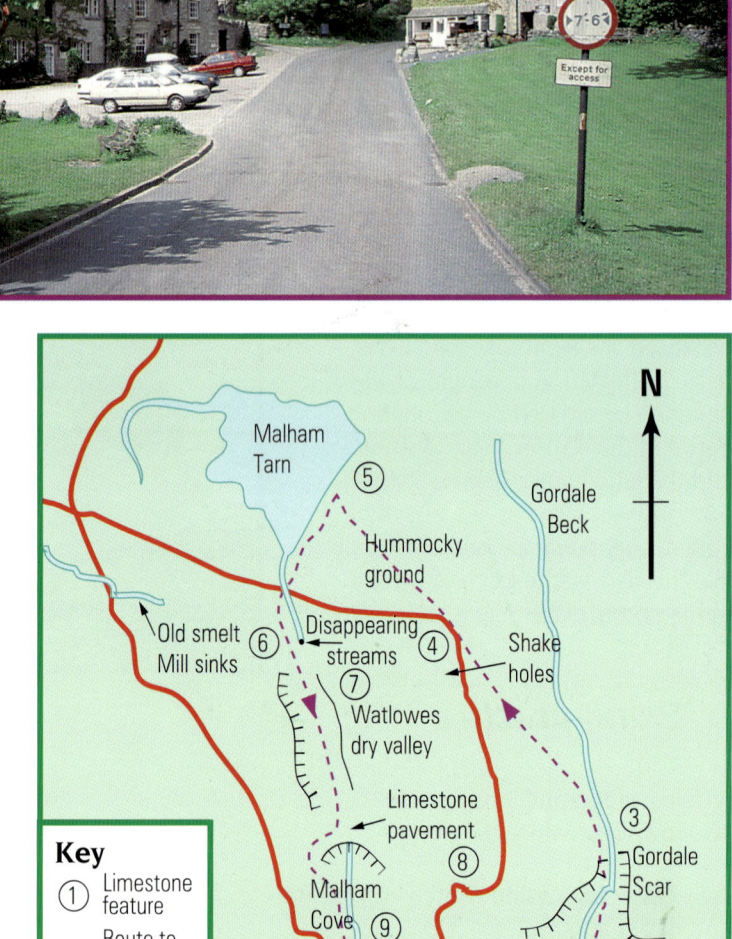

2 The Natural Landscape

National Parks	pp7–8
Honeypot	p38
Accessibility	pp44–5
Quarrying	pp58–61
Tourism	p77

② Janet's Foss

This is a waterfall which has an impressive tufa screen (**C**). Gordale Beck drains from the surrounding limestone area and is rich in dissolved calcium bicarbonate. When the water passes over the end of the falls it causes some calcium bicarbonate to change back to a solid limestone rock (**D**). This is known as tufa.

③ Gordale Scar

It was originally thought that this feature was formed when the roof of an underground **cavern** collapsed. However, due to a lack of rock debris on the floor of the scar, this idea was questioned. It is now more widely believed that Gordale Scar was created during an interglacial period when rapid ice melt provided the waterfall with vast amounts of water causing massive erosion along Gordale Beck (**E**). This area is used by walkers, campers and climbers.

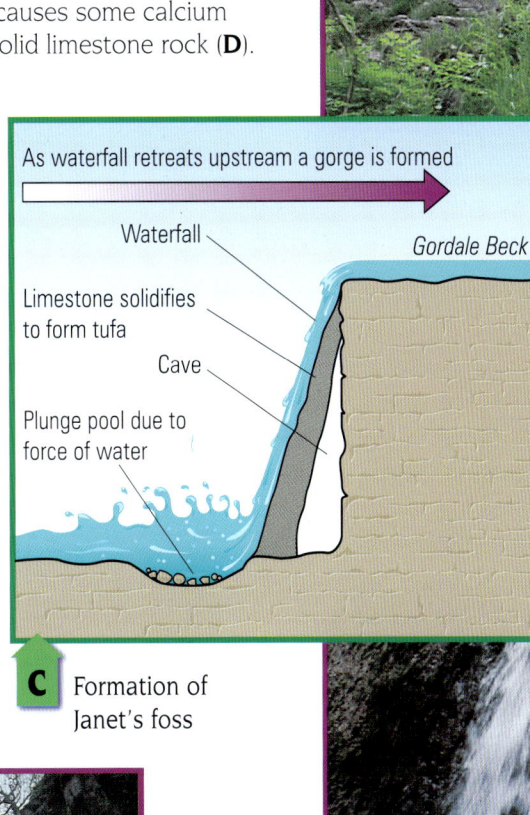

C Formation of Janet's foss

As waterfall retreats upstream a gorge is formed
- Waterfall
- Gordale Beck
- Limestone solidifies to form tufa
- Cave
- Plunge pool due to force of water

D Waterfall and tufa screen at Janet's Foss

④ Shake holes

On the limestone plateau the ground either side of the road is very uneven. This is caused by the development of shake holes which vary in size up to several metres in diameter (see **F** on page 22). The overlying soil is gradually washed downwards into the joints causing the surface to subside.

⑤ Malham Tarn

Despite its name Malham Tarn is not in a corrie. It is located on an area of impermeable slate, dammed by moraine that was deposited by ice at the end of the last Ice Age. This moraine gives the area a hummocky appearance (**F**).

E Gordale Scar and waterfall

21

Themes and Issues: National Parks in the UK

F Cross section of the Malham area

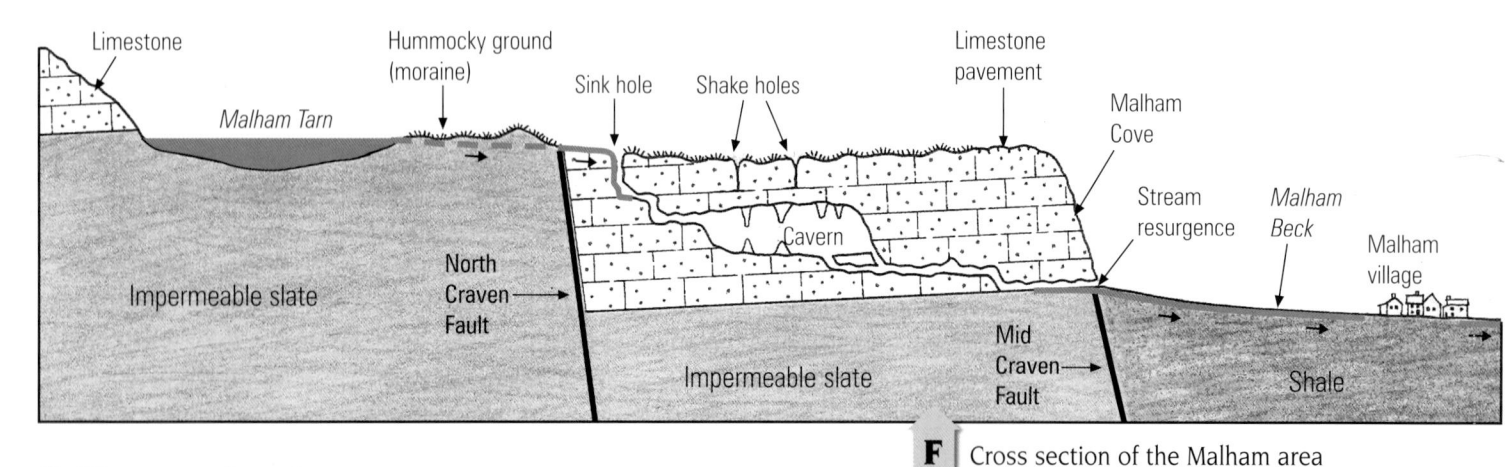

⑥ Disappearing streams

The stream from Malham Tarn flows overland for approximately 500 metres before it sinks into the ground. This is known as a sink hole (**G**). Subsurface drainage is common in limestone areas due to the joints and bedding planes which allow the water to move underground. The water continues to dissolve the limestone underground creating a network of **caverns**.

As the water seeps through the roof of a cavern it evaporates leaving a small deposit of limestone. If this continues a stalactite forms. As water drips off the end of the stalactite onto the floor a shorter, thicker stalagmite is formed. If these two join, a column or pillar is created.

The stream from Malham Tarn reappears to the south of Malham village at the Aire Head spring. The river that appears at Malham Cove is actually from water sinks at the Old Smelt Mill.

G Stream disappearing down a sink hole

⑦ Watlowes dry valley

This valley, like many others in limestone areas, no longer has a river flowing through it. At the end of the last Ice Age when the ground was still frozen a river flowed over the surface. The valley was eroded in the usual way. When the temperatures increased the ground thawed to allow the river to sink into it and flow underground.

Watlowes dry valley is also asymmetrical in shape. The south facing side has a gentler slope than the north facing side. This is due to freeze–thaw activity on the north facing side as it received less sunshine. On the south facing side the top layers of the ground thawed in the day time allowing it to move downhill (**H**).

H Watlowes dry valley

I Formation of a limestone pavement

⑧ Limestone pavement

The limestone pavement started to form 12 000 years ago when the ice retreated exposing bare rock (**J**). The limestone was then susceptible to weathering along the joints and bedding planes. Carbonation weathered the joints to become grykes. The remaining rectangular shaped block became known as a clint.

The limestone pavement is continuously being weathered. When water collects on the surface of a clint a solution hollow may form. As this is enlarged it may be channelled into a solution groove. This erosion continues over the side of the clint and the feature eventually becomes a flute (**I**).

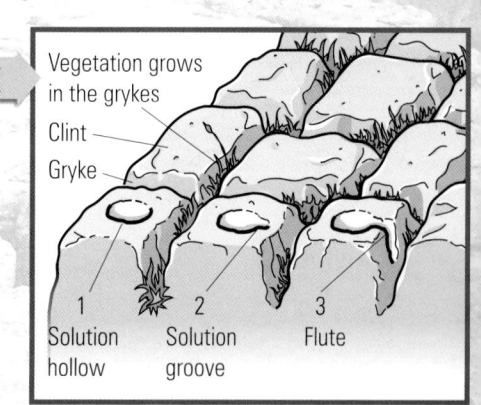

⑨ Malham Cove

Malham Cove is rounded with steep sides and was formed by the large amounts of water flowing down Watlowes valley towards the end of the last glaciation. The stream from the Old Smelt Mill re-emerges from the limestone at the bottom of the cove as it is forced to the surface by a layer of impermeable rock. This is known as a resurgence (**K**).

As the cove and pavement are visited by thousands of people each year, well defined paths and steps have been built to protect the landscape. This is an attempt to make the features easily accessible. They are built out of local limestone to blend in with the scenery. The cove is also popular with climbers.

J Limestone pavement at the top of Malham Cove

Malham Beck emerging from the cove **K**

Issues in the limestone landscape

The stone trade

The limestone pavements provide habitats for many rare and colourful plants. They are being destroyed to provide rockery stone to garden centres around the country. A campaign has been set up by the Yorkshire Dales National Park Authority to make people aware of where this 'water worn stone' is coming from. If the demand for it continues the limestone pavements will rapidly disappear. The National Park Authority is able to make Limestone Pavement Orders which forbid unauthorised removal of the stone. Under these orders 18 areas of limestone are now being protected.

Park and ride schemes

The Yorkshire Dales National Park suffers from much traffic congestion on the narrow windy lanes. The National Park Authority is keen to reduce the environmental effects of congestion. A **park and ride scheme** has been introduced which operates from the Upper Wharfdale valley ten kilometres to the east of Malham. This operates on Sundays in the summer months. The National Park Authority is also encouraging the use of public transport in the park. There is already a frequent bus service to provide access to the Malham area. As an incentive all National Park guided walks are free for those who arrive by public transport.

Exam practice

1 Describe the appearance of limestone pavement and explain its formation. *(6 marks)*

2 **a** Describe the course of the stream from Malham Tarn. *(3 marks)*
   b Explain why this stream disappears and then reappears. *(3 marks)*

3 Explain how caves are formed in areas of limestone rock. Illustrate your answer with diagrams. *(6 marks)*

4 Name two leisure activities that make use of limestone scenery. *(2 marks)*

5 Some residents of Malham village think that tourism is good for the area whilst others think there are too many visitors. Explain how people can hold such different views. *(5 marks)*

6 Name and locate a natural environment that you have studied. For your chosen area explain how the rock type has influenced the landforms. *(8 marks)*

Rivers, water supply and management

Rivers have helped shape the landscape of all the National Parks and provide a good opportunity to study the influence of humans. People have an ever increasing demand for water which has led to the development of many reservoirs. Some rivers provide important wildlife habitats and valuable opportunities for leisure.

A The River Breamish

The Breamish valley, Northumberland

The River Breamish flows off the upland area of Northumberland National Park. The river starts high up beneath the Cheviot Mountain and flows east towards the North Sea, joining the River Till and then the River Tweed before entering the sea (**A**). Like many other rivers the Breamish displays a number of characteristic features along its course.

B Waterfall in the upper valley

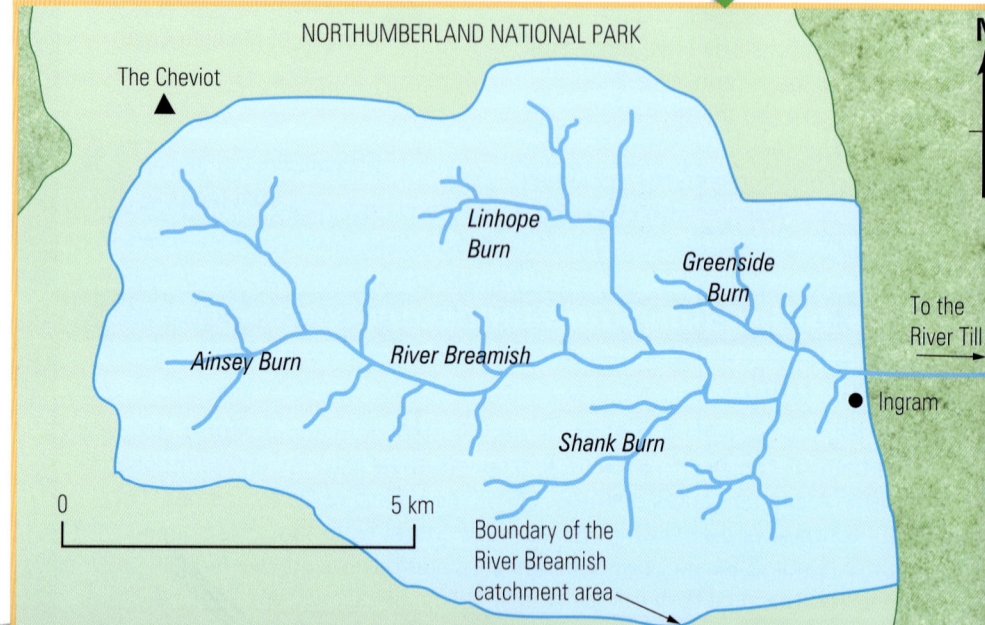

The upper Breamish valley

The source of the Breamish is high up on the moorlands where a large amount of rain falls. This water descends rapidly over the granite hills to collect in narrow channels. The Breamish here is dictated by the contours and **spurs** of the landscape. The river cuts down into the ground by **vertical erosion**. Along these upland stretches waterfalls can be found (**B**) where active vertical erosion is taking place. Erosion on the river bed is mainly by abrasion (the river bed and banks are eroded by the material carried by the river) and hydraulic action (the force of the water acting on the bed and banks). Material that is eroded is carried downstream to be deposited elsewhere.

24   The river starting to erode sideways **C**

2 **The Natural Landscape**

National Parks pp7–8
Nant Ffrancon pp12–13
Accessibility pp44–5
Tourism pp76–84

The middle Breamish valley

As the Breamish works its way downhill it has started to use its energy to erode the sides of the river; this is known as **lateral erosion**. The river has created a flood plain on either side of the channel. The river meanders across this flood plain although it is still confined to a large extent by the steep slopes of the valley (**C**).

Meander in the lower valley **D**

The lower Breamish valley

The lower part of the Breamish has a much wider valley and the flood plain opens out (**D**). The river winds its way across this area and **levées** are built up at the sides. The Breamish has developed many meanders in this area with their characteristic river cliffs and slip off slopes (**E**). It is in this stage that the river has started to deposit its load and **braiding** of the channel occurs. The Breamish leaves the National Park at Ingram and flows north to its confluence with the River Till.

Human activity and the Breamish

The Breamish valley became a popular area for taking day trips from the growing cities on Tyneside. Families would come to the valley to escape urban life and spend the day relaxing. Today the valley receives 100 000 visitors a year. There is a National Park Centre at Ingram where trails into the area can be started. The main economic activity in the area is sheep farming and much of the land is privately owned. The National Park Authority has enabled visitors to gain greater access into the hills by coming to **Access Agreements** with landowners.

E The formation and characteristics of a meander

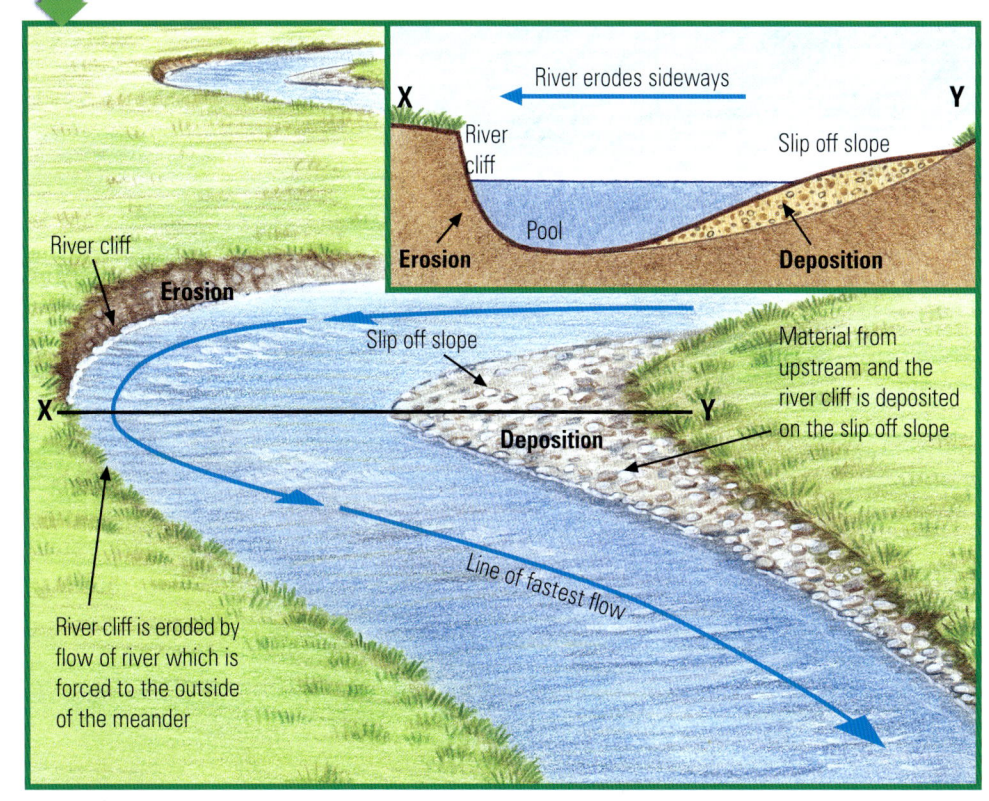

- River erodes sideways
- X — River cliff — Pool — Erosion
- Y — Slip off slope — Deposition
- River cliff — Erosion
- Slip off slope
- Material from upstream and the river cliff is deposited on the slip off slope
- Deposition
- Line of fastest flow
- River cliff is eroded by flow of river which is forced to the outside of the meander

Activities

1. Describe and explain the characteristics of the three stages of the River Breamish.
2. Draw a cross section of a meander and explain the processes that lead to its development.
3. As a research task, find out and then describe how a waterfall forms.

THEMES AND ISSUES: **National Parks in the UK**

Reservoir and water supply in the Peak District

The amount of rainfall varies throughout the year and from area to area in the UK. To be able to provide people with a reliable supply of water, the rainfall needs to be collected in reservoirs. Reservoirs are purpose-built lakes for storing water. The water is passed through treatment plants before being piped to built-up areas.

Howden, Derwent and Ladybower Reservoirs are situated in the Upper Derwent valley in the High Peak of Derbyshire. The valley's location within the Peak National Park has encouraged careful planning and management of the area. It is a working landscape that not only supplies water but has farmland, wildlife habitats and provides recreation.

Why a new reservoir system was needed in the Peak District

The Peak District is surrounded by a number of large industrial cities. At the end of the nineteenth century the rapid growth of these cities and an increasing population led to a greater demand for water. A new water supply was needed.

A joint water board was formed between Derby, Nottingham, Leicester and Sheffield. In 1901 and 1916 two dams were built to create Howden and Derwent Reservoirs. In 1945 a third dam was completed to create Ladybower Reservoir (**F** and **G**). The villages of Derwent and Ashopton were evacuated before being flooded. A new village was built to rehouse these people and employees of the water board. Since 1974 the reservoir and water works have been the responsibility of Severn-Trent Water.

F The Upper Derwent reservoirs
(Source: Peak Park Authority)

Why the Upper Derwent valley was chosen

- The Derwent valley was deep and narrow at certain points so it was easy to construct the dams needed.
- Steep sides allowed a large capacity of water to be stored.
- The area was composed of gritstone, therefore water could not seep through the valley floor.
- The high annual rainfall, with an average of 1350 millimetres per year, gave a reliable input of water.
- The Derwent had a large upland catchment area which enabled a large amount of water to be stored.
- The moorland catchment area was virtually uninhabited, therefore the water was not contaminated.
- The area provided soft water for industrial processes.
- It was located relatively close to the areas of demand and was high up so the flow was by gravity.

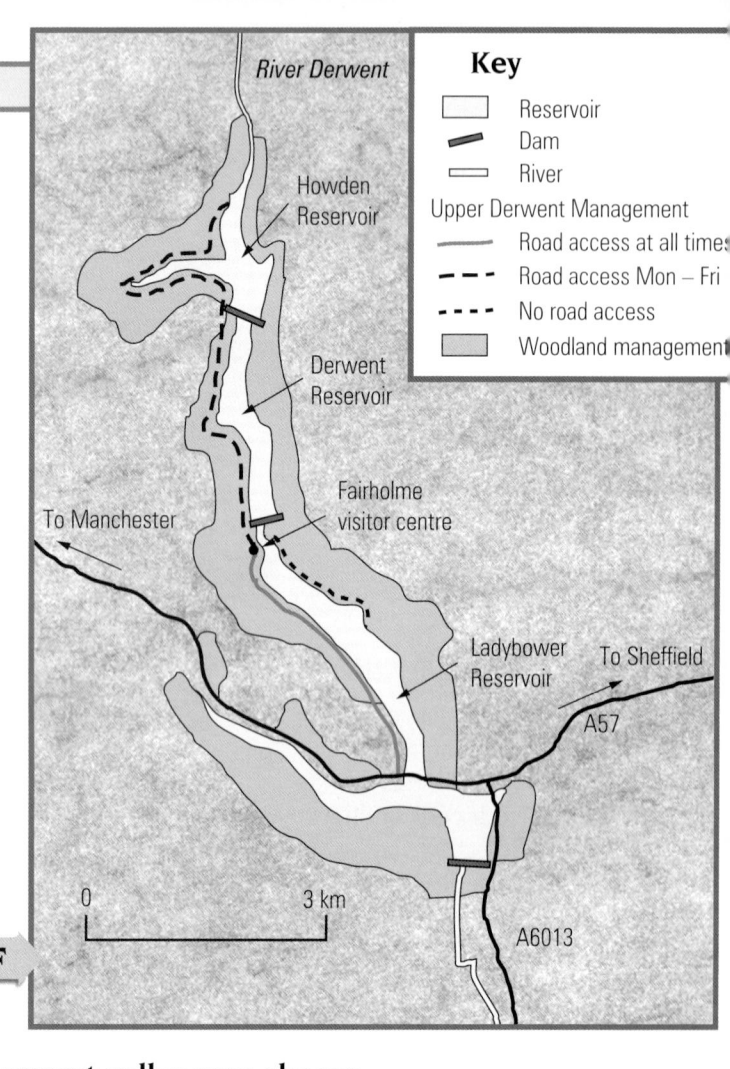

G Ladybower Reservoir

2 The Natural Landscape

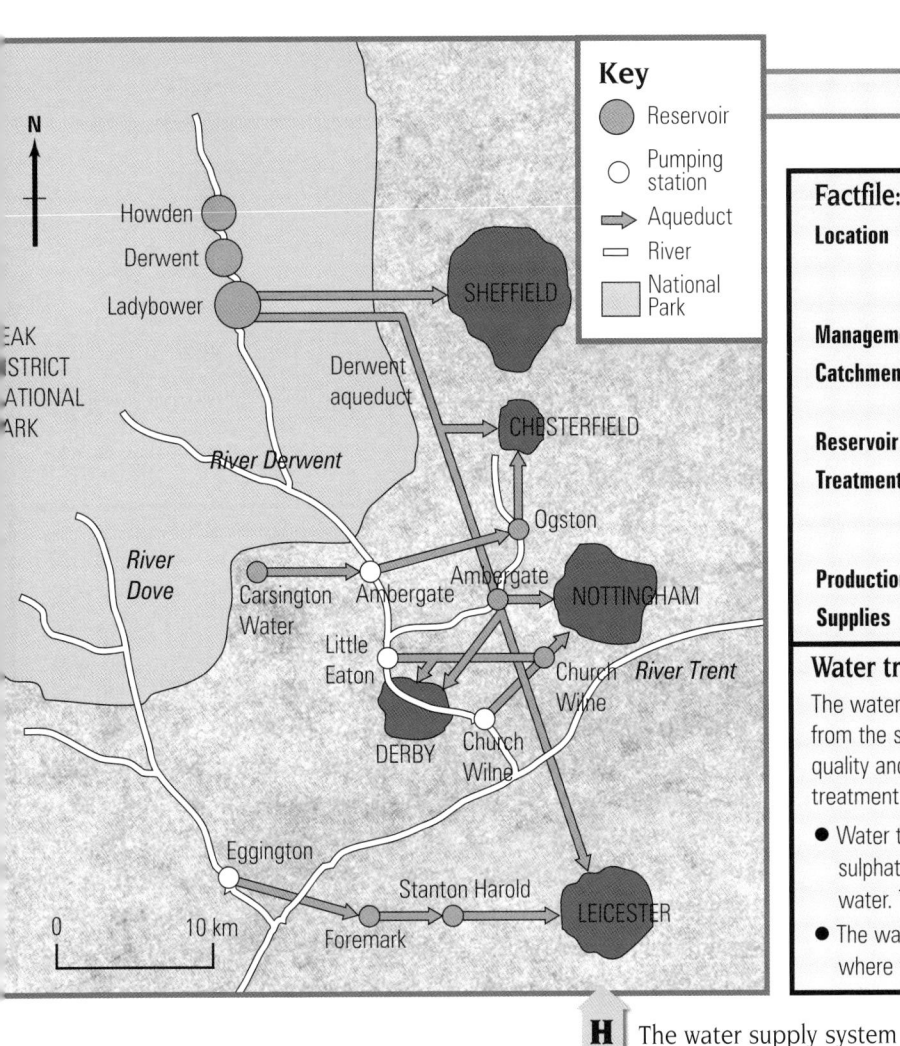

Factfile: The Upper Derwent reservoirs

Location	Howden, Derwent and Ladybower Reservoirs are situated in the Upper Derwent valley in the High Peak of Derbyshire
Management	Severn–Trent Water
Catchment area	19 850 hectares which includes the feeder rivers Ashop, Derwent, Alport and Noe
Reservoir capacity	Total capacity 463 692 million litres
Treatment works	Water is filtered, chlorine added and pH (a measure of acidity in the water) corrected at Yorkshire Bridge or Bamford
Production	225 million litres of water a day
Supplies	Leicester, Nottingham, Sheffield and Derby (**H**)

Water treatment

The water in the reservoirs is naturally acidic and brownish in colour from the surrounding **peaty** area. It needs to be cleaned to meet strict quality and safety standards. A number of processes are involved in the treatment of water:

- Water travels down three aqueducts into a well where lime and ferric sulphate are added. The lime neutralises the natural acidity of the water. The ferric sulphate causes the peat particles to join together.
- The water and chemicals are mixed as they flow along a channel where the peat forms a solid.
- The water flows upwards through concrete tanks in the process of clarification. Peat forms a layer of sludge at the surface which is then removed.
- More lime is put into the water and chlorine added which is a disinfectant.
- The water passes through filters which are composed of sand and anthracite. This removes any remaining particles. Excess chlorine is then removed.
- The water is then ready for the consumer in the urban areas (**H**).

H The water supply system
(Source: Severn–Trent Water)

Woodland, wildlife and farming

Severn-Trent works with the National Park Authority and other local bodies in order to enhance the beauty of the area. Much of the surrounding moorland is a **Site of Special Scientific Interest** due to the presence of rare birds and plants. Large areas of conifers were planted around the reservoirs to keep animals away from the water's edge and reduce pollution. These are now being redesigned to include a larger number of broadleaf trees which will give the area a more natural appearance and a greater variety of wildlife.

Recreation in the valley

The Upper Derwent attracts over 1.25 million visitors each year. In 1980 the Upper Derwent Partnership was formed representing various interests in the area, such as the Peak National Park Authority, Severn-Trent Water and Forest Enterprise. An information centre has been built at Fairholme to inform the public about the area they are visiting. As part of the management scheme a **park and ride** operates at certain times of the year when access to some roads is limited (**F**). A number of activities are encouraged in the area:

- walking - a good network of footpaths is found in the area around Fairholme. These are aimed at different levels of ability from low level paths by the water to the more difficult uphill woodland paths.
- Cycling - a cycle hire centre at Fairholme is in operation which has proved to be very popular.
- Horse riding - throughout the area there are many kilometres of bridleways.
- Fishing - trout fishing on Ladybower and Derwent Reservoirs is allowed with a permit. Rowing boats can be hired for fishing.

Activities

1. Suggest why dams and reservoir schemes are not always welcome by everyone.
2. Describe the role of a water company in providing a reliable supply of water and in protecting the surrounding area.
3. In 1995 the UK suffered from a major drought. Use any resources available, for example the library, CD-ROM, newspapers, to write a report. In your report mention the reasons for the drought and the short- and long-term effects.

Themes and Issues: **National Parks in the UK**

A threatened wetland – the Broads

The Broads consist of over 200 kilometres of navigable open water along the River Yare and its tributaries (**Ia**). The area has 25 freshwater lakes or broads and is surrounded by fen and marshland. The whole area is of international importance for its wildlife and many rare species of plant. In 1987 the Broads became the first **Environmentally Sensitive Area** (ESA) in Britain and in 1989 was recognised as the eleventh National Park in England and Wales. The area now attracts over a million visitors each year who come to boat, walk, fish and sightsee.

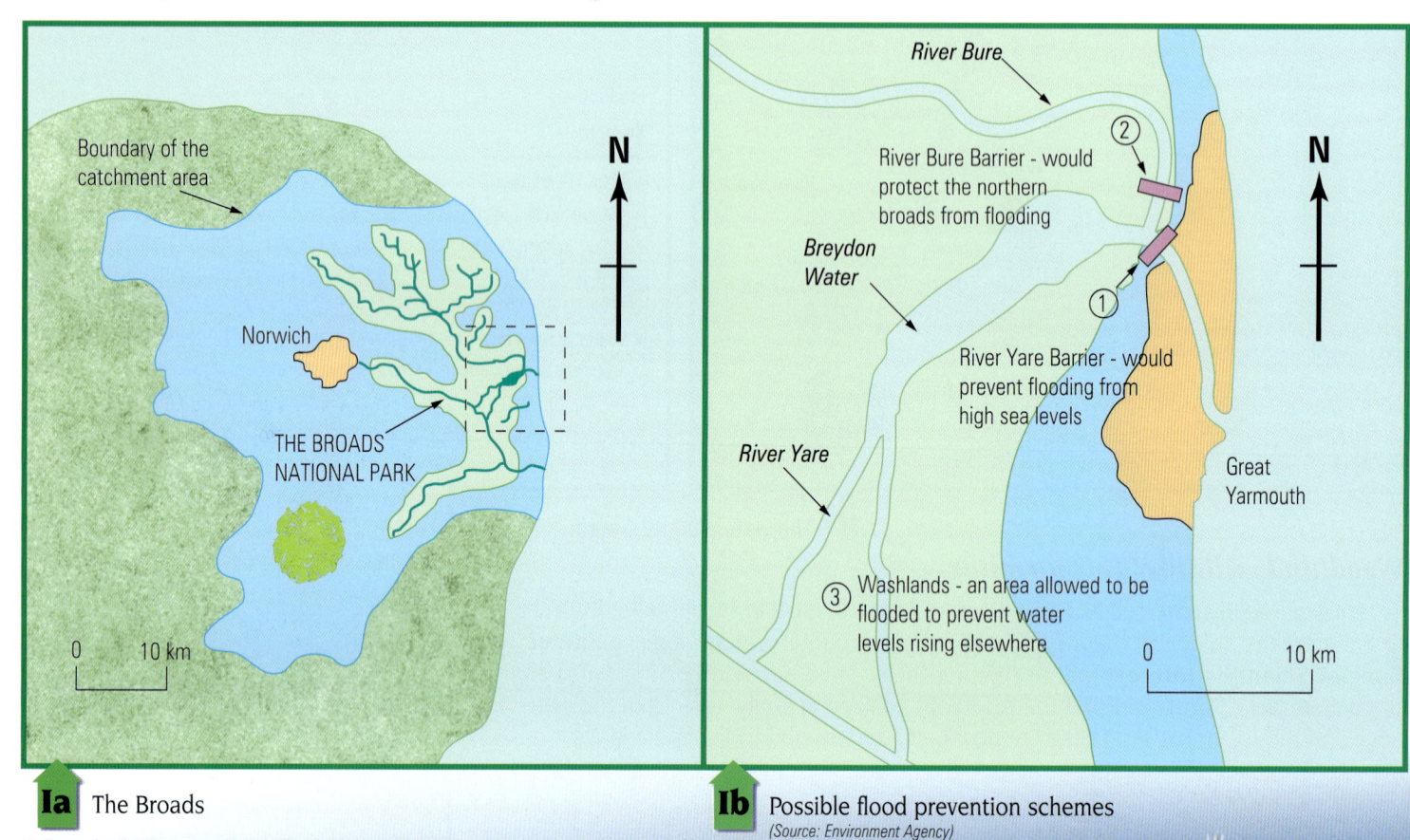

Ia The Broads

Ib Possible flood prevention schemes
(Source: Environment Agency)

Flood defence in the Broads

In January 1953 a deep depression moved down the North Sea resulting in a **storm surge**. Onshore winds, a high **spring tide** and intense low pressure caused the level of the sea to rise. The effect of this was catastrophic in the confined coastal areas along eastern England and the Netherlands. In the Thames estuary the sea level rose by three metres. In eastern England over 200 people died, livestock drowned and there was massive devastation of property.

Major flood protection schemes were introduced after further floods in 1976 and more recently in February 1993, when a spring tide caused a surge of water two metres in height up the River Yare. Many of the banks were breached with damage estimated at £500 000.

Flood protection schemes were introduced by the National Rivers Authority, now the Environment Agency. Since becoming a National Park the Broads Authority has also worked closely on these schemes (**Ib**). It has strengthened over 240 kilometres of existing river embankment at a huge cost. A programme has been set up to maintain these defences. This will cost approximately £63 million over the next ten years.

2 The Natural Landscape

Issues in the Broads

Farming in the Broads

The Broads have supported human activity for over 500 years. During this time the area has been used for grazing and **peat** has been extracted from the marshland. Much of the grazing land in the marsh has been upgraded so it can be used for more profitable agricultural practices. Farmers were given grants from the European Union's Common Agricultural Policy to drain and convert the marsh into land suitable for growing cereal crops. In an attempt to control this the Broads were designated an **Environmentally Sensitive Area** to encourage the traditional farming methods of grazing animals on freshwater marshes.

With the trend towards arable agriculture, farmers have treated the crops with chemicals to increase yields. However, some of the chemicals are washed into the Broads causing major pollution. The phosphate and nitrogen in these fertilisers coupled with sewage is causing the process of **eutrophication** to occur. This will eventually lead to deterioration of water quality in the Broads. One way the Broads Authority is dealing with the problem is to dredge the river bed and place the earth that is recovered on the banks where it can help to form fertile soil.

Tourism in the Broads

Tourism brings money into the local economy but there are often negative effects. The huge increase in tourism has put a great deal of pressure on the quiet rural villages. More facilities have been provided such as houseboats, chalets and additional services. These developments have not always been in keeping with the character of the area.

Boating on the waterways has become a popular holiday pursuit. Unfortunately, damage caused by the boats to the river banks is a major problem (**J**). In places the banks have been eroding back at a rate of up to three metres in ten years. The river banks are particularly vulnerable as they contain important wildlife and plant habitats. With bank erosion the surrounding farmland may be prone to flooding. In 1992 lower speed limits were introduced of as little as five kilometres per hour in certain areas. Strict fines are imposed on people who break this speed restriction. The Broads Authority is also trying to educate visitors so that they realise the potential problems of boating in this **wetland**. As part of the overall strategy of flood protection the banks are continually being repaired and strengthened.

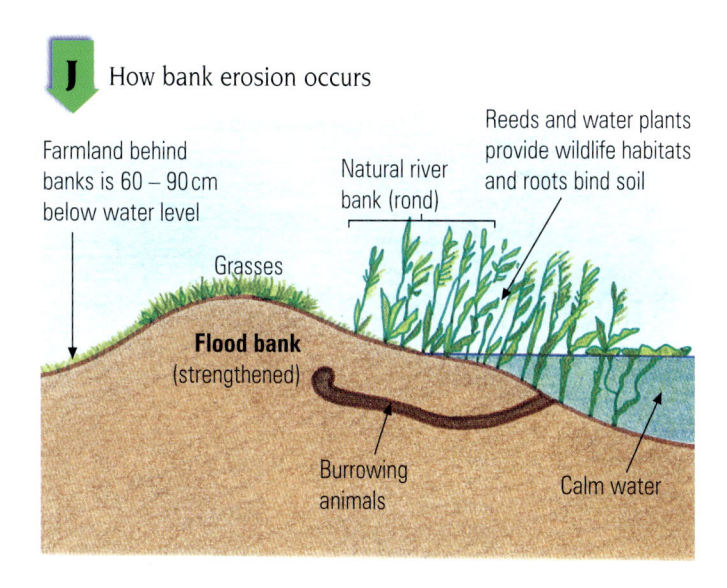

J How bank erosion occurs

a Natural river bank

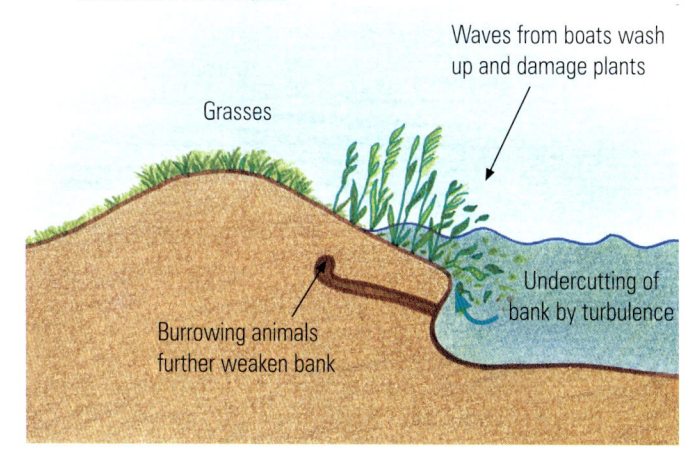

b River bank suffering from erosion
(Source: Broads Authority)

Activities

1. The Broads have been an agricultural area for hundreds of years. Describe the changes that have taken place in farming and discuss the problems that have arisen.
2. What is the impact of tourism on the Broads?
3. With reference to an area you have studied, explain why flood defence schemes are needed.

Woodland and forest management

Woodlands and forests are the natural vegetation of the UK and so are an important part of the landscape. Many of the National Parks contain large areas of semi-natural woodland, but there are increasing amounts of land being converted to plantation woodland.

An ancient woodland - the New Forest

The New Forest was created in 1079 by William the Conqueror as a Royal Hunting Ground. The area contains a variety of habitats which are the result of the interaction between people and the physical landscape. It retains much of its original character and today receives over 7 million visitors a year. The New Forest was one of several areas which had been suggested as an additional National Park. In 1994 it was decided that the New Forest would not be given National Park status. Instead it was to remain a **Heritage Area** with similar powers to a National Park (**A**).

The New Forest and surrounding area **A**

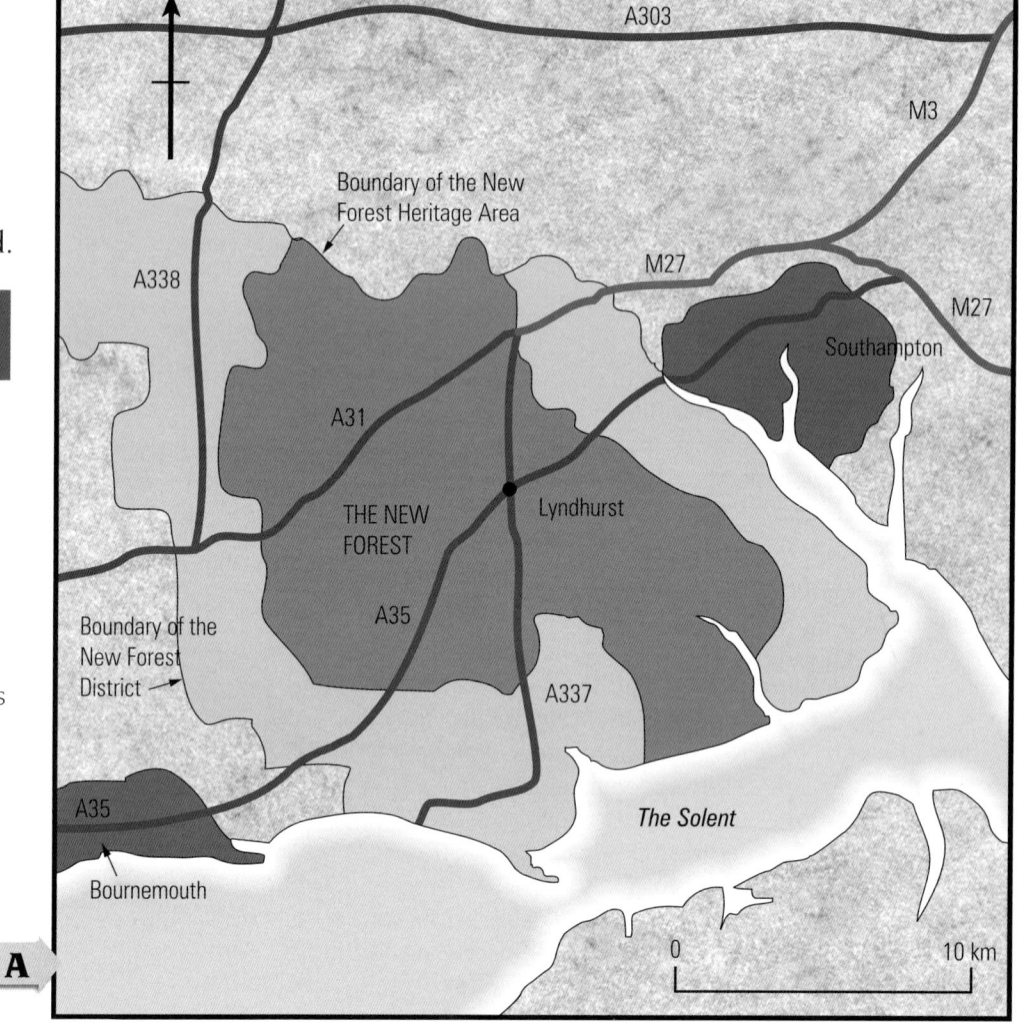

In 1974 the New Forest District was created and administered by the district council. The Heritage Area is contained within the District boundary and covers 376 square kilometres (about 58 000 hectares). This area is now run by the New Forest Committee. Three main types of habitat are found in the area (**B**):

- Heathland - these areas of heather support a range of birds, reptiles and butterflies.
- Valley bogs - there are a large number of valley mires (bogs) which provide important **wetland** habitats for both plant and wildlife.
- Ancient broadleaved woodland - the main trees found are oak, beech and sycamore. Some of these trees date back to the seventeenth century. These areas provide ideal environments for lichens, fungi, mosses and ferns which support a wide variety of insect species.

2 The Natural Landscape

Highway strategy pp44–5
Tourism pp76–84

The New Forest is owned by the Forestry Commission and by private landowners. A large proportion of the land is used as 'open forest' which is available for grazing animals. Much of this is covered by heathland and grasses. In the enclosed land where soils are more fertile some trees, mainly conifers, are commercially grown. There are also areas of ancient broadleaved woodland (**B**).

Landowners, known as Commoners, in the area are entitled to graze their animals in the New Forest for a small fee. This tradition dates back to the mediaeval period. The animals, mainly ponies, cattle, donkeys, sheep and pigs, are allowed to roam throughout the 'open forest'. There are over 300 Commoners who use the land this way. The area also supports wild deer.

The Heritage Area is administered by the New Forest Committee. The committee is made up of members who represent various bodies who have an interest in the forest (**C**). The job of the committee is to promote the conservation of the traditional practices of the area whilst balancing the natural and human forces that determine the character of the forest.

B Types of land use in the New Forest
(Source: Forestry Commission)

LAND OWNED BY FORESTRY COMMISSION
- Open Forest 31%
  - Grassland with bracken and gorse
  - Heathland
  - Valley bogs and wet heathland
  - Broadleaved woodland
- Enclosed Forest 15%
  - Broadleaved woodland
  - Coniferous woodland

PRIVATE LAND 54%
- Agricultural, residential and private commons

TOTAL AREA 58 000 hectares

Forestry Commission: manages land and recreation, including conservation

Hampshire County Council: planning of minerals and roads in the area

Country Landowners Association: a number of councils work with the committee

English Nature: promotes understanding of the countryside and manages Sites of Special Scientific Interest

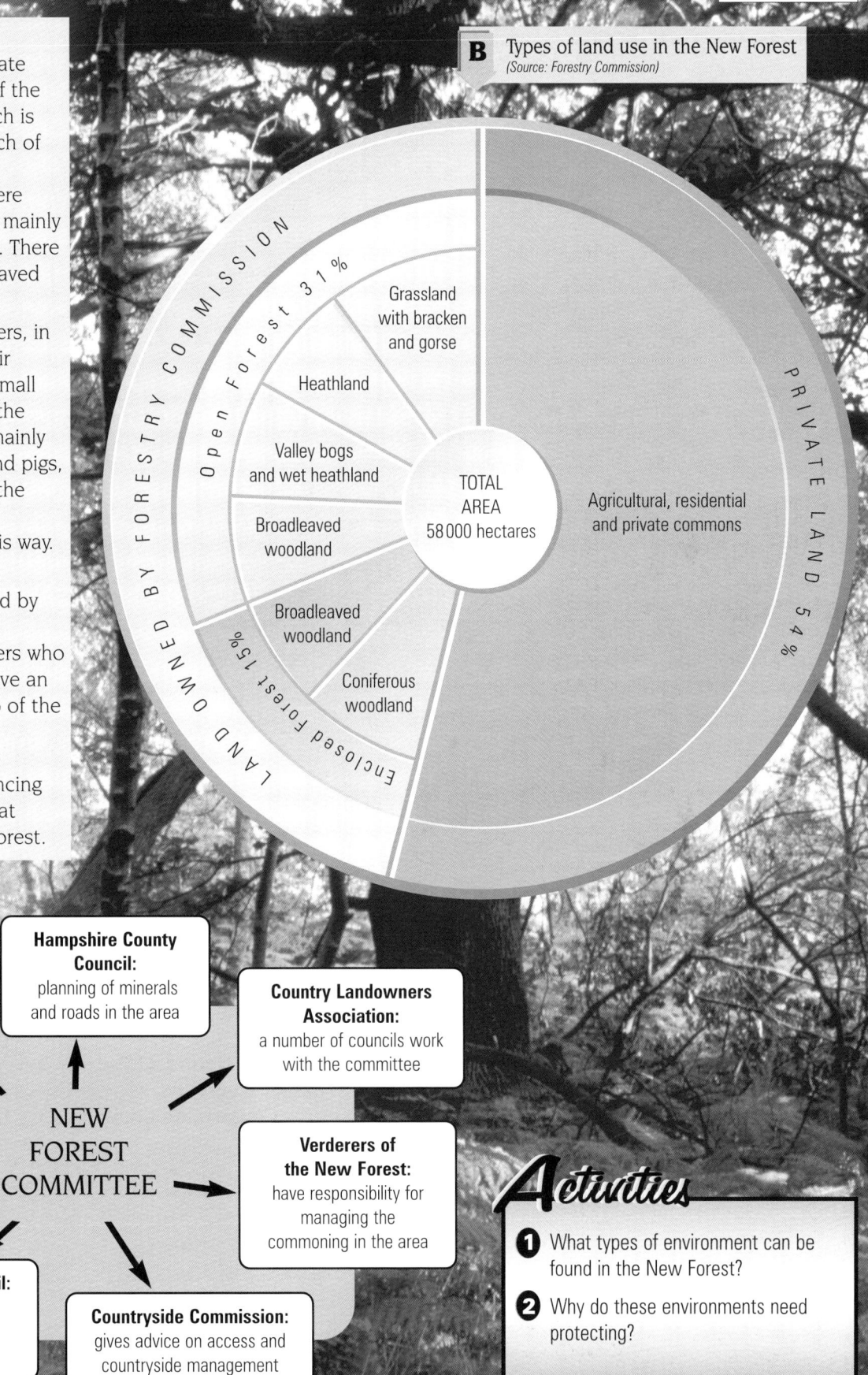

NEW FOREST COMMITTEE

Verderers of the New Forest: have responsibility for managing the commoning in the area

New Forest District Council: management of tourism and development; also provides community services

Countryside Commission: gives advice on access and countryside management

Activities

1. What types of environment can be found in the New Forest?
2. Why do these environments need protecting?

C The administration of the New Forest

31

Themes and Issues: **National Parks in the UK**

Issues in the New Forest

There are a number of issues which the New Forest faces. It is a highly accessible area and has become more popular in recent times.

Tourism

The majority of visitors arrive in the area by car. This has caused increased traffic congestion especially at the more popular locations. A highways strategy has tried to limit some of these problems. Facilities have been built to accommodate visitors, such as 143 car parks with the larger ones having picnic sites, toilets and paths.

There are now ten camp sites which have been designated to control camping. Before 1971 camping was permitted anywhere (**D**).

Tourism in the area is also highly seasonal with the greatest pressure in the summer months. The area has benefited greatly from tourism as over £66 million is spent by visitors each year. The increase in demand for facilities has also created a further 5000 new jobs.

Development

Because of its popularity the New Forest has faced pressure from development. Around the New Forest is a buffer zone. There is great demand for this land for building, especially in the east. This could pose a serious threat to the area's wildlife and vegetation. The A31 which runs through the New Forest has been made into a dual carriageway and linked to the M27. The population of the area has increased to 170 000 and about 20 000 new homes have been built.

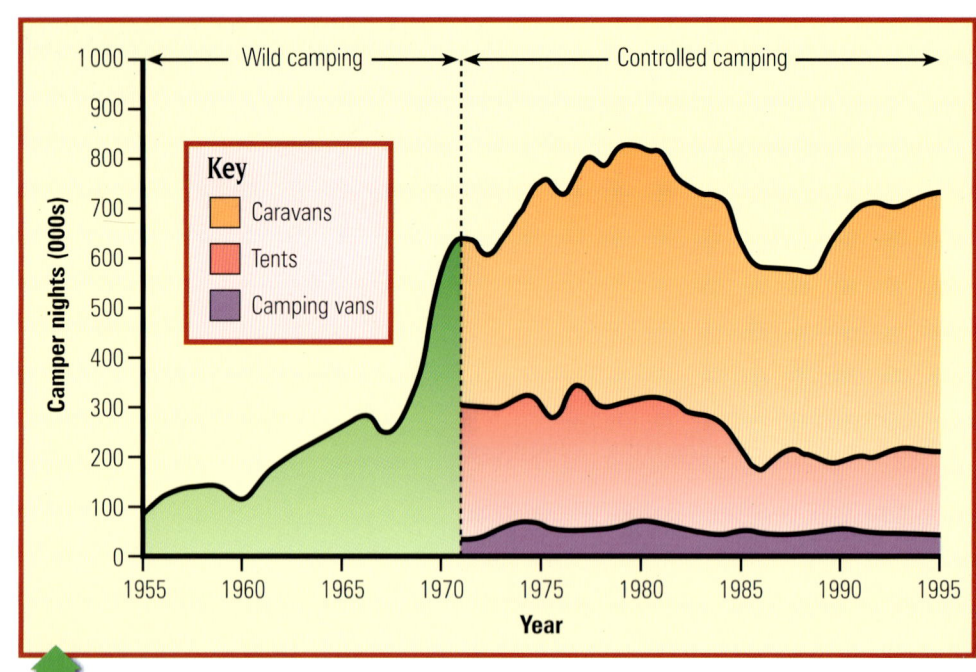

D Recreational pressure - camping in the New Forest
(Source: Forestry Commission)

Protecting the New Forest landscape

The New Forest has been recognised, both nationally and internationally, as an area in need of protection. Various pieces of legislation have been implemented to manage the area:

- New Forest Acts - a number of acts have been passed to protect the different landscapes within the area.
- **Sites of Special Scientific Interest** (SSSI) - there are 14 SSSIs within the New Forest Heritage Area which are controlled by English Nature. These sites have limited public access.
- National Nature Reserve - in 1969 the Forestry Commission agreed with English Nature to give the New Forest the status of a National Nature Reserve.
- Wetland of International Importance - in 1993 the New Forest Heritage Area was recognised as having important **wetland** areas.
- Special Protection Area - in 1993 the EU Wild Bird Directive gave protection to a number of bird species and their habitats.
- **Area of Outstanding Natural Beauty** (AONB) - on the southern fringe of the New Forest 32 kilometres of coastline has been designated an AONB. This is controlled by the **Countryside Commission**.
- Countryside Heritage Sites - Hampshire County Council has identified 37 Heritage Sites within the New Forest.

2 The Natural Landscape

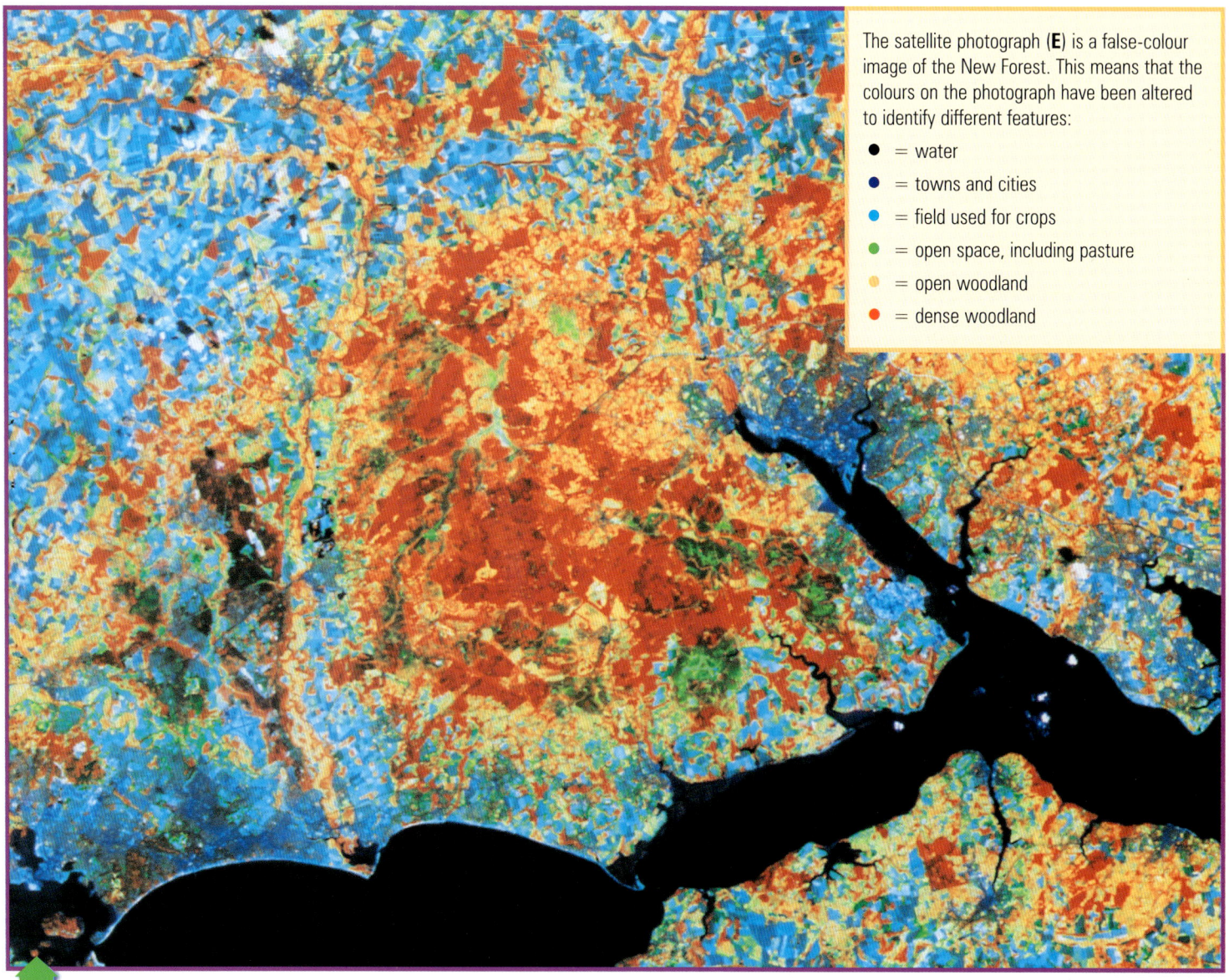

The satellite photograph (**E**) is a false-colour image of the New Forest. This means that the colours on the photograph have been altered to identify different features:

- ● = water
- ● = towns and cities
- ● = field used for crops
- ● = open space, including pasture
- ● = open woodland
- ● = dense woodland

E Satellite image of the New Forest and surrounding area

Activities

Use the satellite photograph (**E**) and map (**A** on page 30) of the New Forest to answer the questions. You may also need an atlas.

1 Draw a map of the New Forest and mark on the following features. Use different colours to show the features:
- the boundary of the Heritage Area;
- the area of dense woodland;
- open woodland;
- pasture;
- fields being used for crops;
- the Solent, the Isle of Wight, Southampton and Bournemouth.

2 Describe the distribution of human activity, such as settlement, farming and forestry, in the area on the satellite photograph.

3 What problems have the increase in visitors to the New Forest brought? How have the New Forest Committee tried to overcome them (see also **C** on page 31)?

4 Why do you think the New Forest was not given National Park status?

33

THEMES AND ISSUES: **National Parks in the UK**

A plantation forest by Loch Lomond

The Loch Lomond Regional Park is an area of largely unspoilt mountains surrounding a loch. The park covers 44 200 hectares of land and Loch Lomond is Britain's largest lake (33 kilometres in length and seven kilometres at its widest point). Forest covers about 15 per cent of the park (**F**). Most of this is coniferous plantations where trees are commercially grown. This is known as afforestation. There are also areas of historic broadleaved woodland. Land use in the area is mainly agricultural, with sheep farming on the steeper ground and beef and dairy farming closer to the loch.

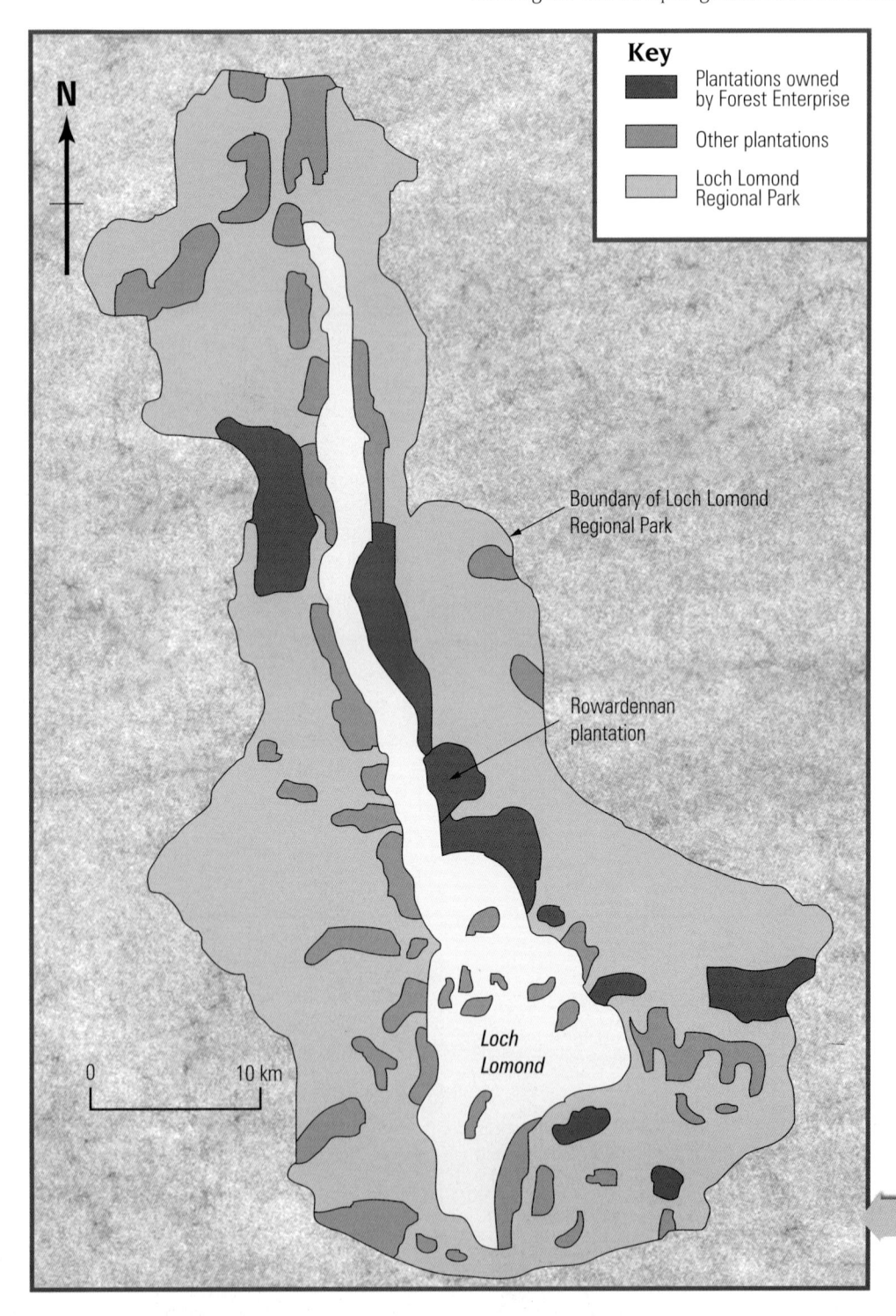

Loch Lomond is the most visited area in Scotland due to its location close to the cities of Glasgow, Edinburgh and Stirling (containing 2.6 million people). The area is managed by Loch Lomond Regional Park Authority which has overall responsibility for the landscape. Many environments within the park have also been protected. The park is a National Scenic Area and an **Environmentally Sensitive Area**. There are 20 **Sites of Special Scientific Interest** (SSSI) and 253 hectares of **wetland** around the loch.

Forest Enterprise

Within the Loch Lomond Regional Park the largest amount of commercial forest is owned by Forest Enterprise, which is part of the Forestry Commission. This totals 3300 hectares of land around the loch. It is mainly coniferous forest but some is ancient broadleaved forest. Within the next ten years up to 300 hectares of coniferous forest are expected to be felled. This will be the biggest potential for change in the landscape that the area will have to face so careful management is needed.

F Forests around Loch Lomond
(Source: Loch Lomond Regional Park)

2 The Natural Landscape

Forest plantation at Rowardennan

The plantation is located on the eastern shores of Loch Lomond and covers 1000 hectares of land. It is the largest plantation owned by Forest Enterprise. The forest is dominated by a variety of coniferous trees. There is also oak forest and some open space (**G**). Half of the forest area has been designated an SSSI as part of a larger protected area.

The forest was managed for about 250 years by the Duke of Montrose until it was taken over by the Forestry Commission in 1951. Between 1951 and 1969 part of the original oak forest was underplanted with conifer trees. Conifer trees are quick growing and have a wide range of uses. Over the next five years 60 000 tonnes of timber are expected to be harvested. This will be used for:

- construction timber;
- pallet wood;
- chipwood;
- pulpwood for mills.

Underplanting with coniferous trees has caused some loss of broadleaved trees due to the competition for light and nutrients. The conifer trees can also destroy the undergrowth and make the soil in the forest more acidic. Clearance of the coniferous trees now encourages natural regeneration of native broadleaved trees. The long-term aim is to diversify the age and number of tree species within the plantation. With the increase in the variety of habitats and wildlife it is hoped to give the plantation a more natural appearance.

Increased tourism in the area has put further pressure on the forest. The West Highland Way runs through the forest and attracts 100 000 walkers each year. There is access to the surrounding mountains, such as Ben Lomond. The area provides accommodation to visitors (hotel and youth hostel) and there are camp sites by the loch. The eastern shore road (B837) runs through the forest and has car parking, whilst on the loch shore there are boating facilities.

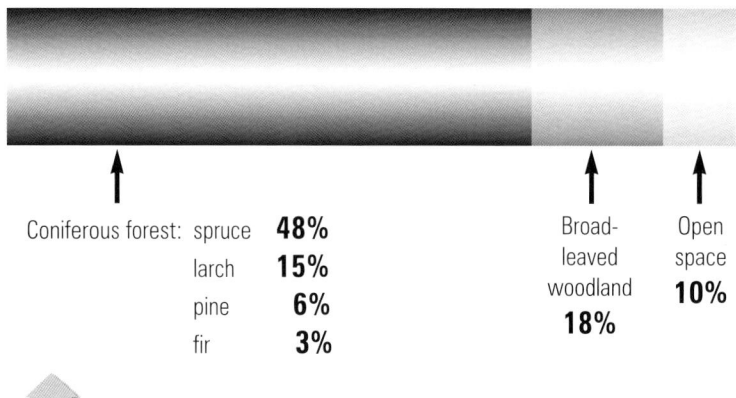

Coniferous forest: spruce **48%**
larch **15%**
pine **6%**
fir **3%**

Broad-leaved woodland **18%**

Open space **10%**

G Types of land use in the plantation at Rowardennan
(Source: Forest Enterprise)

Activities

1. How does afforestation affect the natural environment?

2. How would each of the following affect forestry in the Loch Lomond Regional Park:
   a increased recycling of paper;
   b increased use of imported wood;
   c increased use of home produced wood?

3. For a named example describe the location and characteristics of a forest plantation. What pressures are placed on the plantation?

4. Upland areas are sometimes said to be threatened by activities such as afforestation. Why would some people feel threatened by this?

3 THE HUMAN LANDSCAPE

National Parks were inhabited long before they were designated as protected areas. Therefore settlement and access to these areas have always been key features in the landscape. Settlement patterns and road transport networks continue to change and develop over time.

Settlement patterns in National Parks

A The shape of settlements

Many settlements in National Parks originated hundreds of years ago and have become an important feature in the physical landscape.

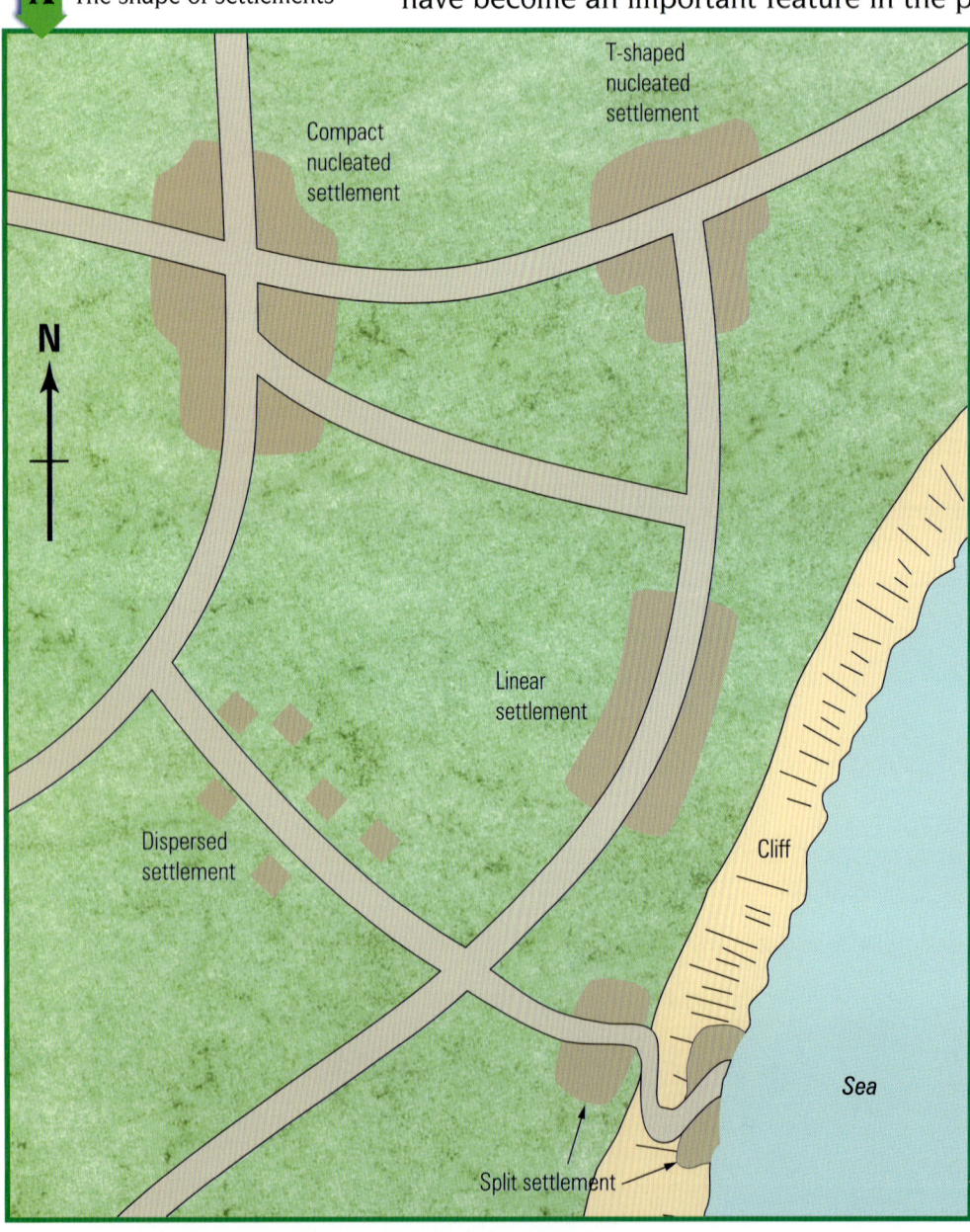

Labels on map A: Compact nucleated settlement; T-shaped nucleated settlement; Linear settlement; Dispersed settlement; Cliff; Sea; Split settlement

Settlements vary considerably in size. A farmstead is an individual house surrounded by the farm buildings. A hamlet is two or three houses located together, whilst a village is a number of houses with some services. Towns are much larger settlements that provide many more services.

Settlements became established in areas where people's basic needs were met. Factors influencing the location of settlements included a reliable water supply, a source of fuel and sites that were easily defended. These factors can help to explain the pattern of settlement that is seen today.

Many terms are used to describe settlements. These include:

- Site - the original area of land on which the settlement was built.
- Situation - the position of the settlement in relation to the surrounding area.
- Function - the reason why it developed, for example a settlement may have been established because of the success of its market. The function may have changed over time and as a settlement has developed.
- Shape or pattern when seen on a map (**A**) - the shape can be influenced by the site that it occupies and natural and human routeways.

3 **The Human Landscape**

Castleton pp38–43
Tourism pp76, 80–81
Exmoor pp85–9

An OS map extract from the North Yorkshire Moors **B**

Activities

Study the OS map extract of the North Yorkshire Moors (**B**) and answer the following questions:

1 a What were the advantages for the location of Runswick Bay (810161)?

b What facilities are provided for visitors in Runswick?

2 What are the settlement shapes for the following villages: Runswick (810161), Mickleby (803129), Goldsborough (835147) and Ugthorpe (798112)?

3 a At what height is Northfields Farm (808143)?

b Why are there no settlements in grid square 7712?

4 What is the distance to the nearest half kilometre from the centre of Runswick to the centre of Lythe following the B road and the A174?

5 a Copy out and complete table **C**. Rank the villages in order of importance by identifying the number of facilities in each of the settlements.

b Explain why some settlements have developed to offer more facilities than others.

SETTLEMENT	P	▲	🚐	☀	✝ Inn/PH	☎	P	Sch	Number of A roads	Number of Minor roads	Other	Total facilities	Rank position
Lythe (845132)													
Goldsborough (835147)													
Hinderwell (794165)													
Runswick (810161)													
Ugthorpe (798112)													

C Facilities offered in settlements

37

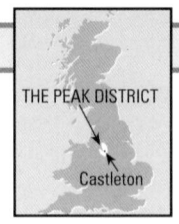

Castleton – a honeypot village

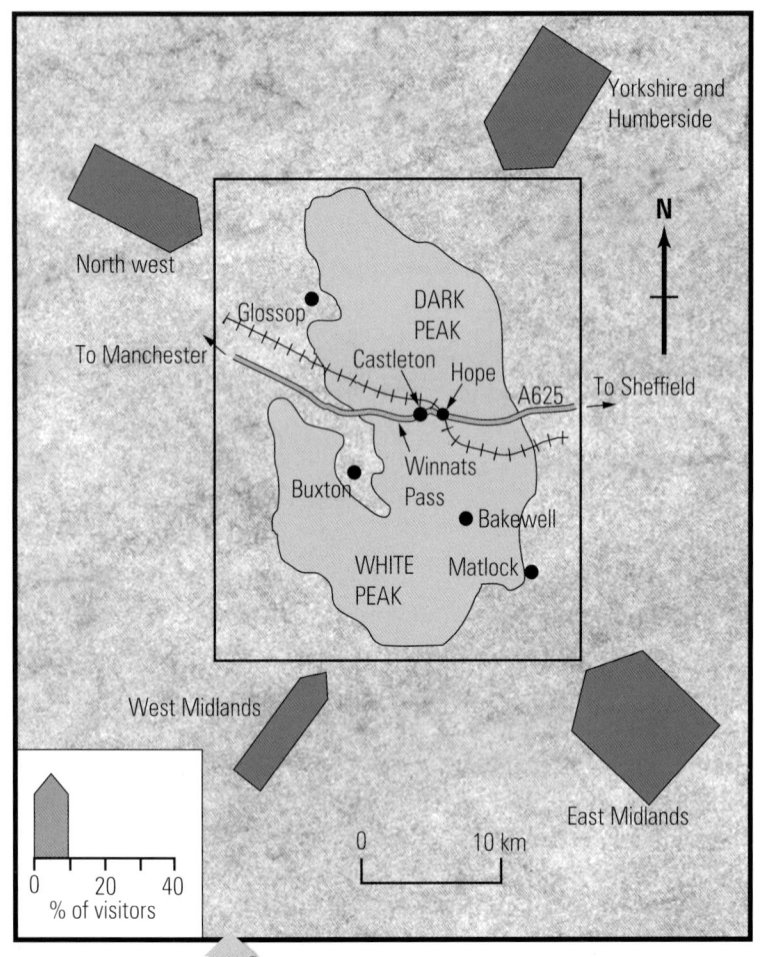

Castleton is the most visited settlement in the Peak National Park. It is an example of a **honeypot**; this is an area that attracts thousands of tourists each year.

Half the population of England lives within 95 kilometres of the Peak District. Castleton is situated in the Hope Valley on the boundary between the Dark Peak and White Peak areas (**A**). The Dark Peak area consists mainly of shale and is found to the north, whereas the White Peak area to the south is mainly limestone.

Castleton lies at the western end of the Hope Valley, 16 kilometres from Buxton and 26 kilometres from Sheffield. The A625 passes through Castleton and runs the length of the Hope Valley. This is now closed to the west due to a land slip at Mam Tor. Access to Castleton from the west is only possible by Winnats Pass. This is a spectacular, narrow, steep-sided gorge. The road in the pass also has a steep gradient which, combined with the large number of visitors to the area, creates a bottleneck.

A The location of Castleton and origin of visitors to the Peak National Park
(Source: Peak National Park)

The growth of Castleton

Castleton's original function was one of defence and administration due to its location in an area which was rich in lead. The village gradually developed into a market town as it was on the route for salt being brought from Cheshire to Sheffield. In 1894 a railway line opened between Manchester and Sheffield which stopped at Hope, two kilometres from Castleton. This opened the way for the growth of tourism in the village.

Land use and employment

Castleton has a growing population. In 1951 there were 650 people living in the village; by 1991 there were 689 people. There are still a number of farmers in the local area who have mixed and dairy farms. There are also quarry workers and many people earn a living from tourism. The occupations of people in the village are given in **B**. This shows that over half the people living in the village are

Managers and professional workers **53.4%**

Other non-manual workers **24.9%**

Manual workers **15.1%**

Others **6.6%**

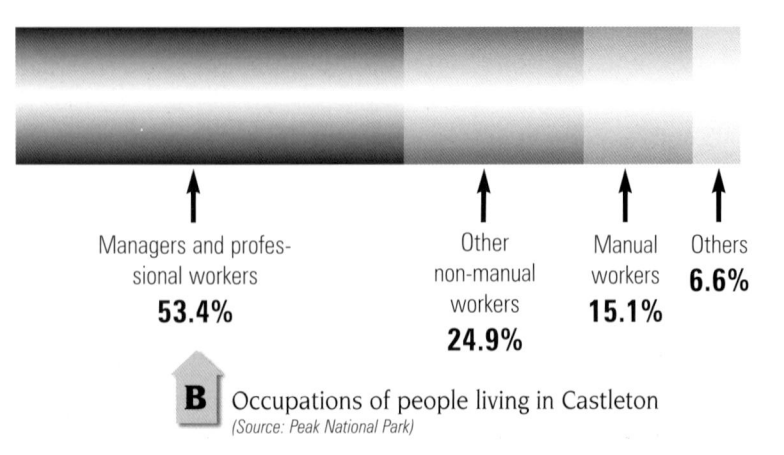

B Occupations of people living in Castleton
(Source: Peak National Park)

38

3 The Human Landscape

Settlement pp36–7
Accessibility pp44–5
Tourism pp76–84

Key
- Residential
- Tourist
- Local
- Both tourist and local

Land use in Castleton

C Land use and services in Castleton

Services In Castleton

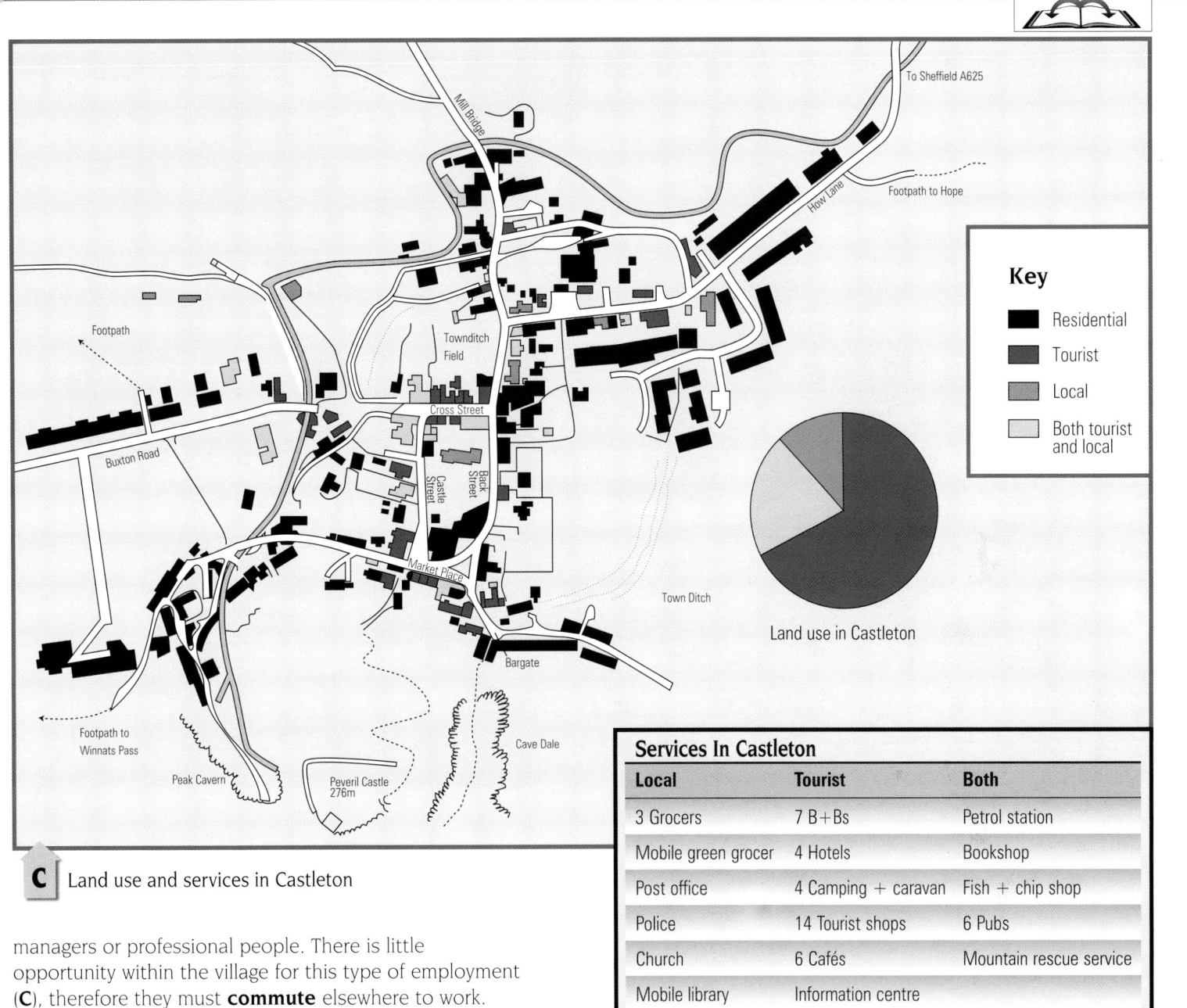

Local	Tourist	Both
3 Grocers	7 B+Bs	Petrol station
Mobile green grocer	4 Hotels	Bookshop
Post office	4 Camping + caravan	Fish + chip shop
Police	14 Tourist shops	6 Pubs
Church	6 Cafés	Mountain rescue service
Mobile library	Information centre	

managers or professional people. There is little opportunity within the village for this type of employment (**C**), therefore they must **commute** elsewhere to work.

Major employers in the area:

- Hope Cement Works, owned by Blue Circle, employs 300 people, 90 per cent of whom are local.
- Interconnect Products Limited supplies electronic equipment and employs 179 people, 63 per cent of whom are local.
- Thermal Measurements electronics company employs 21 people, most of whom are local.
- Losehill Hall employs 40 permanent staff, most of whom are local people, and also many seasonal staff.

Activities

1 Why does the Peak National Park have a high number of visitors?

2 Which area do the majority of visitors to Castleton come from (see **A**)?

3 Look at the land use map and table (**C**).
  a What is the percentage of tourist based services and local based services?
  b Describe the distribution of the local services?

  c What conflicts could arise from the number of services provided?
  d Why is there a high concentration of tourist shops at the junction of Bargate and Market Place?

4 a Why do an increasing number of people commute to work?
  b What problems might this cause for Castleton?

Themes and Issues: *National Parks in the UK*

D OS map extract from the Castleton area

Attraction	Grid reference	Information
Speedwell Cavern Treak Cliff Cavern Blue John Cavern Peak Cavern	139827 136832 132833 147827	Many of the best caves in Britain can be found in the Castleton area. These show caves allow visitors to enjoy the spectacular scenery without special equipment or training. They display a range of limestone features such as stalagmites, stalactites and columns.
Mam Tor	127836	This is known as the Shivering Mountain and is popular with walkers. It is very distinctive as half the mountain has slipped away due to the soft shale rocks.
Peveril Castle	149826	The castle was built in 1086 on the top of a hill overlooking the Royal Forest.
Castleton Village	150829	Within the village are the Castleton Village Museum and numerous gift shops selling Blue John stone. This stone is mined in the area and is blue and yellow in colour. Its name originates from the French for these colours.

E Attractions in Castleton

40

3 The Human Landscape

Tourism in Castleton

Castleton was an established tourist centre 400 years ago and was even visited by Mary Queen Of Scots. Tourism in the area is not new. Today people visit Castleton for various reasons:

- Tourists browse in the many gift shops and stroll around the village.
- They visit the caverns, castle and museum (**E**). The number of people who visit the caves or castle is small compared to those visiting the village. However, the caves and castle remain amongst the ten most visited attractions in the Peak District.
- Outdoor activities are popular in the area. Edale marks the beginning of the Pennine Way which is the start of many walks and hikes. Other activities include climbing, mountain biking and hang gliding.
- School parties carry out fieldwork in the area.

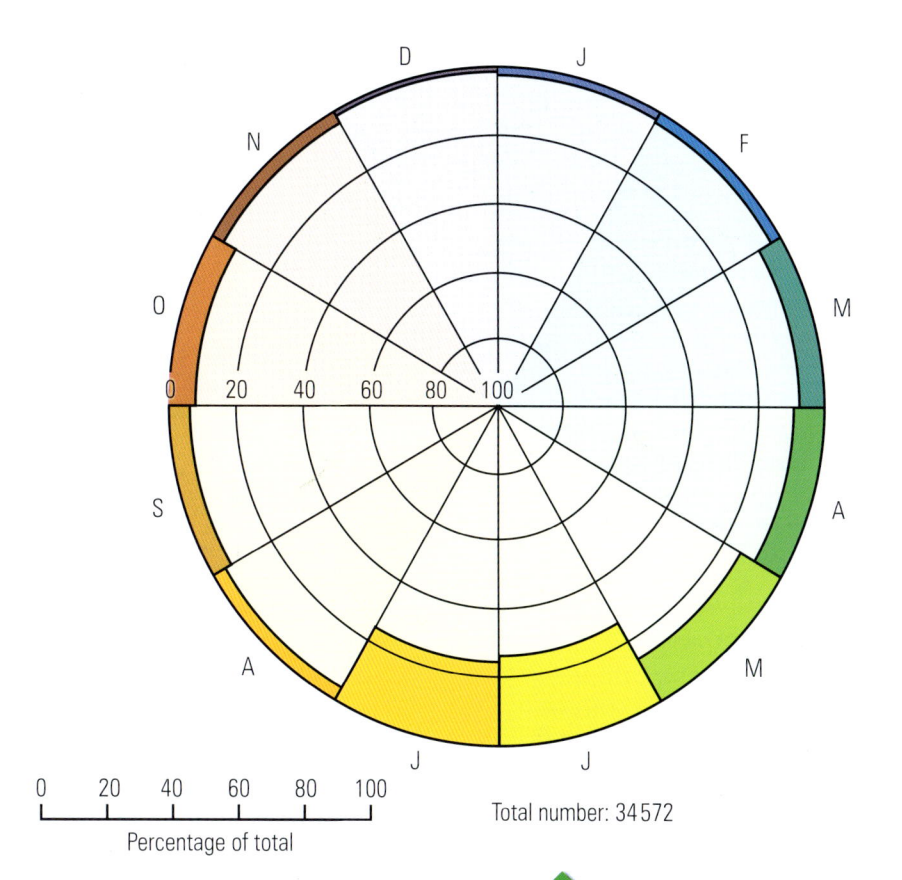

Total number: 34 572

F Seasonal trends of visitors to Castleton

Seasonal trends in tourism

Surveys have shown that Sunday is the most popular day for visiting Castleton. In May 1990, 1631 vehicles were recorded on a Saturday whereas on the Sunday 2719 were recorded. People generally stay less than two hours and so there is a quick turnover of people. A survey carried out in June 1994 showed that the majority were day visitors from the surrounding conurbations. Only one person in ten stayed overnight. **F** shows that the most popular months were June and July and the least popular was December. Such a strong seasonal pattern will affect the income of people working in the village.

Activities

Using the OS map extract (**D**) answer the following questions:

1. What forms of transport can be used to visit the village?

2. Why is Castleton a honeypot?

3. What is the land use at the following six-figure grid references:
   a 194854;   b 158817;   c 143836?

4. Give the likely views of the following people on tourism in Castleton:
   a a retired resident;
   b a local farmer;
   c a cavern owner;
   d a young married couple;
   e a National Park representative.

41

Themes and Issues: *National Parks in the UK*

The benefits and problems of tourism in Castleton

The village depends on tourism which generates employment and money for the local economy. As Castleton is a major tourist attraction it creates a certain pride within the settlement. Although tourism is important for the local economy, it has to be balanced with the needs of the villagers.

Employment
Tourism creates many job opportunities for local people. These include retail and the provision of services, e.g. cafés, hotels and bed and breakfast accommodation. This allows local people to work within the area whilst in many other villages people have to move to seek employment.

Economy
The large number of tourists spend money in the village. This creates wealth for the village which can be ploughed back into the local economy.

POSITIVE EFFECTS OF TOURISM

Conservation
Due to the large number of visitors, people are aware that many sites need to be conserved, e.g. the entrance money to the castle is used to preserve the site.

Regional links
Tourism enables the village to have strong links with the surrounding area. This prevents Castleton from experiencing rural decline (when the number of services decreases as people move away) like many other villages.

G Positive effects of tourism

Congestion
Congestion has created many problems both on the small narrow roads and in the car parks. The large volumes of traffic cause air and noise pollution and can spoil the attraction of the village. Further conflicts arise when visitors park across people's drives. Plans to make the car parks larger will only create even more problems by encouraging more visitors.

Holiday homes
An increase in the number of holiday homes has made house prices in the area rise. Many young people are forced to move away as they cannot afford these inflated prices. This could lead to social unrest between the temporary residents and the local people.

NEGATIVE EFFECTS OF TOURISM

Footpath erosion
A major problem is the erosion of footpaths, especially at Winnats Pass and Mam Tor. Attempts have been made to reduce the impact of visitors by diverting the routes and building stone paths.

Lack of amenities and privacy
Due to the high number of tourist services the basic needs of the local people are not always met. The presence of tourists and large numbers of school parties often leads to a lack of privacy for the residents and an increase in noise in the area.

Crime
There has been an increase in car crime, litter and dog fouling. Acts of vandalism are more frequent, especially on the pay and display metres and public toilets.

H Negative effects of tourism

Exam practice

Diagram I shows sketch maps of a village located within a National Park 30 kilometres from a large town in 1890 and 1990. Diagram J shows how the occupations of people living in the same village in 1890 and 1990 have changed.

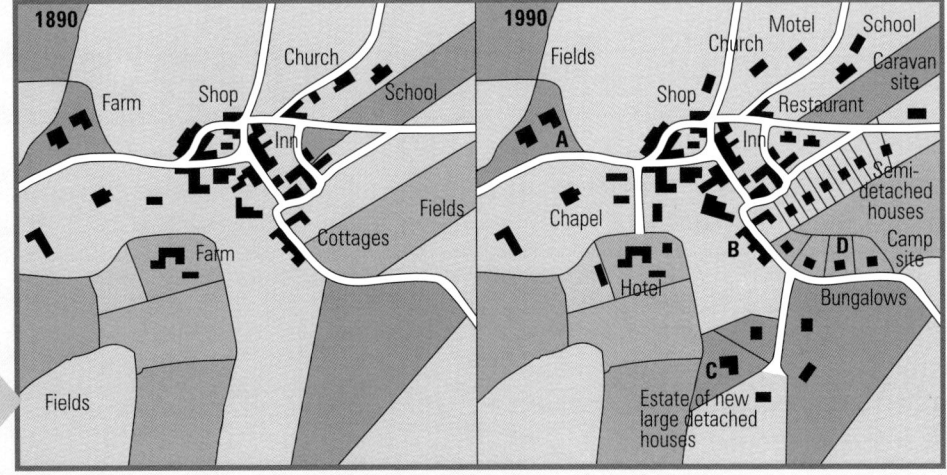

Sketch maps of a village located within a National Park **I**

The occupations of people living in the same village **J**

Study diagram **I** and answer the following questions:

1. Using evidence from diagram **I** describe what changes have occurred in the village. *(5 marks)*

2. Four residential areas are labelled (**A–D**) on the 1990 map in diagram **I**. Copy and complete the table below choosing a residential area for each person. Give reasons for your choice. *(4 marks)*

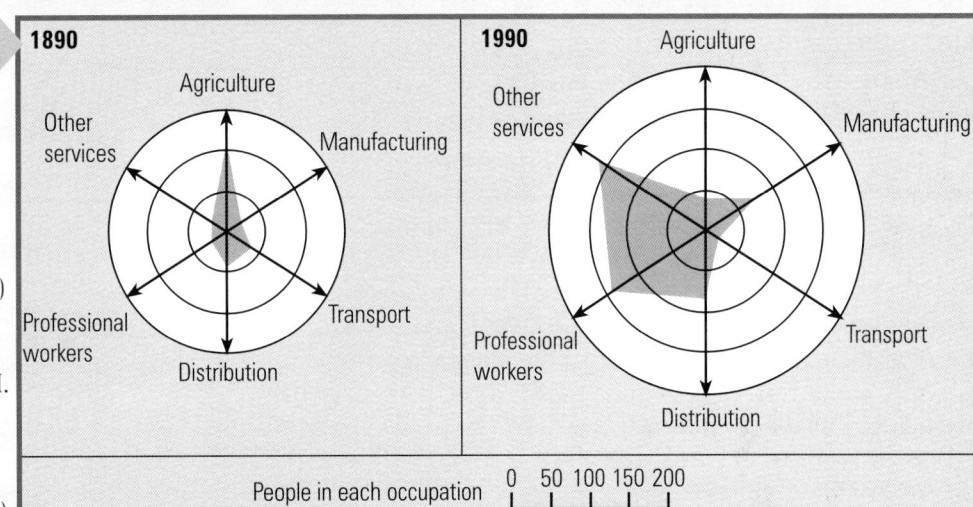

People	Area (A–D) on map	Reason for choice
A bank manager who works in the town		
A retired person		
A local farmer		
A local shop owner		

Study diagram **J** and answer the following questions:

3. What was the main occupation of the people in the village in 1890 and 1990? *(2 marks)*

4. **a** How can you tell that there has been a large increase in the number of people living in the village?

   b Suggest one possible reason for this increase. *(2 marks)*

5. Why has the number of people working in agriculture fallen? *(2 marks)*

6. What benefits and problems do the commuters bring to the village? *(5 marks)*

Accessibility of National Parks

Visitor patterns to National Parks have changed as transport networks have developed. Many parks originally depended on railways for their accessibility. Car ownership has increased since the 1950s which has given people greater freedom. Today 90 per cent of visitors to National Parks travel by car. This is due to the luxury of door to door transport provided by the car which has led to the decline in public transport services.

The development of the motorway network has increased the accessibility of the National Parks (**A** and **B**). Approximately 25 per cent of the UK's population now live within a three-hour drive of a National Park. This has meant that day trips and short breaks have increased in popularity. Some parks such as the Lake District, Yorkshire Dales and Peak District are more accessible and are closer to major centres of population (**A**). These parks therefore receive a larger number of visitors.

Key
- National Park
- Other protected areas
- Large centres of popula[tion]
- Motorways
- Main roads

Major access routes to National Parks **A**

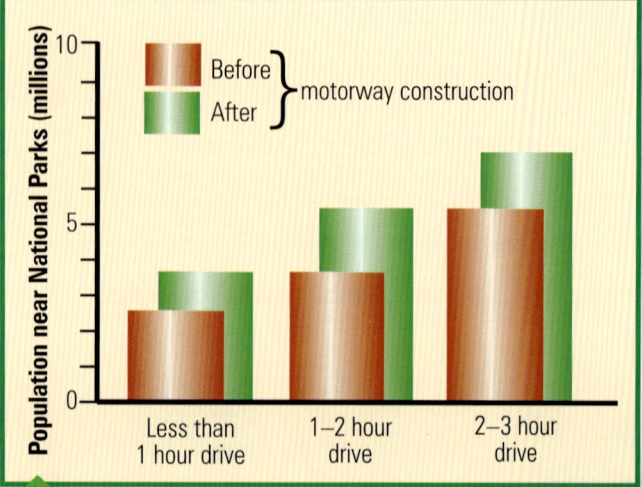

B Road improvements increase the accessibility of National Parks

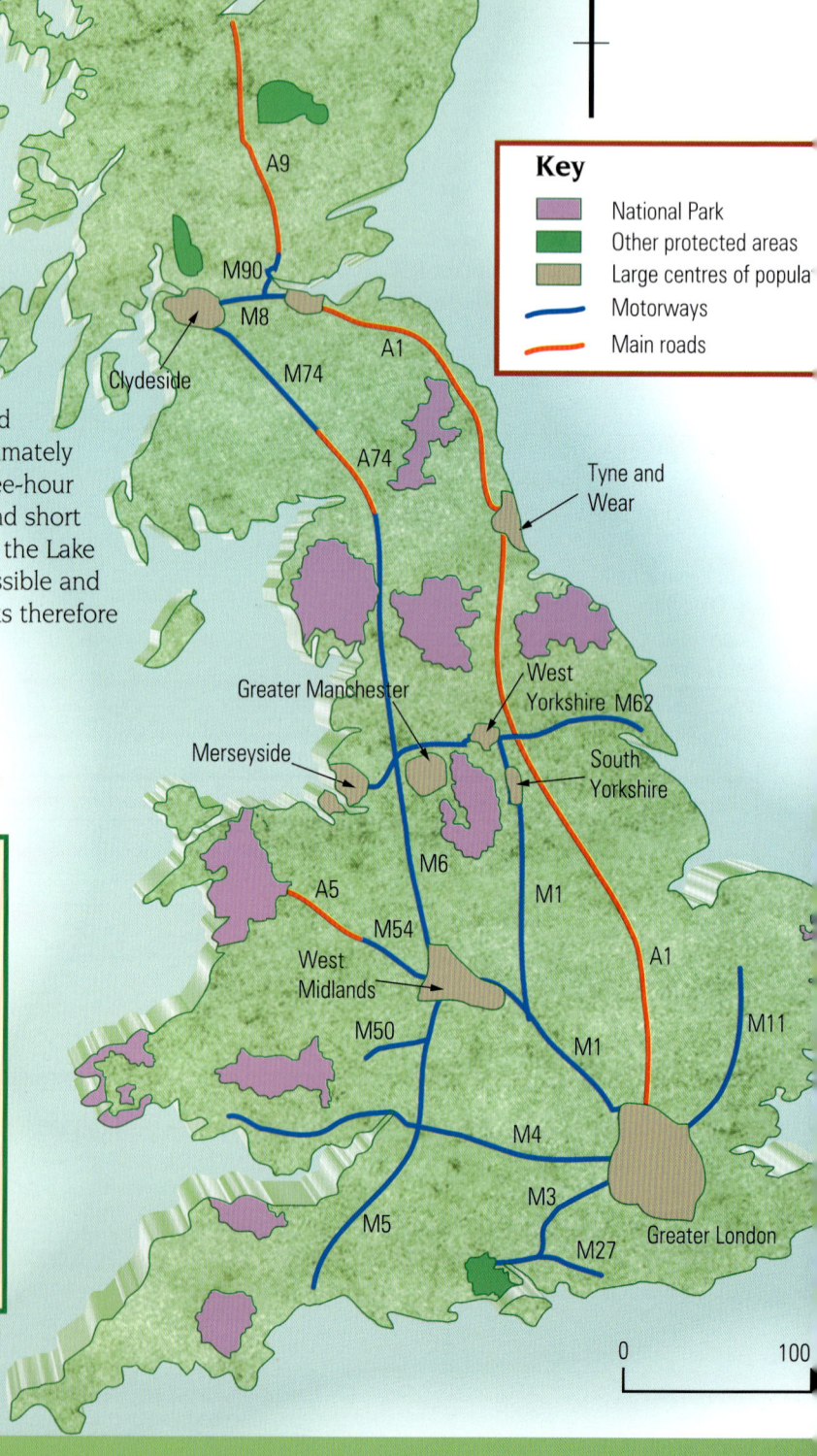

3 The Human Landscape

National Parks pp6–9
New Forest pp30–33
Tourism p76

With the increase in visitors many parks have experienced road congestion. The greater volume of traffic in National Parks has led to many conflicts between residents and visitors. Many parks contain narrow, windy roads and do not have the parking space required. Traffic congestion can reduce the enjoyment of the park areas by increasing air and noise pollution, whilst queues of traffic can be unsightly. Attempts are being made to once again increase the importance of public transport to help reduce the numbers of cars on the roads.

The **National Park Authorities** are not directly responsible for the planning of roads in the parks. This is the job of the local county council. A common response to congestion is to upgrade and widen popular routes. Whilst this eases the flow of traffic, it is a source of much controversy.

A highway strategy for the New Forest

Many of the National Park Authorities have proposed Traffic Management Schemes to try and overcome the problem of traffic congestion. A Traffic Management Scheme has been introduced in the New Forest in an attempt to reduce the number of accidents to the forest animal stock and deer population. These animals have the right of way over the area. A highway strategy was prepared by Hampshire County Council with a number of key aims:

- Visitors to the area are to be made aware that they are entering the New Forest. Information regarding the special nature of the area is to be clearly displayed.
- Within the New Forest **Heritage Area** the roads are classed as:
  – primary through routes;
  – secondary routes;
  – forest byroads.

  Each road receives different planning in accordance with its use. The plan aims to keep long-distance traffic on the primary through routes and off the unsuitable forest byroads. It also restricts the use of some roads to smaller vehicles.

- On unfenced roads speed restrictions are enforced to reduce the number of accidents to animals. The remaining roads have a speed limit of 65 kilometres per hour (40 miles per hour) (**C**).
- Within the New Forest Heritage Area a network of highway signs should be developed which are specific to the area (**C**).

C Sign to enforce speed restrictions in the New Forest

Activities

1. Look at map **A**. Which National Parks are the:
   a most accessible;
   b least accessible?

2. If you lived in London what route would you take to:
   a Snowdonia National Park;
   b The Cairngorms Regional Park?

3. Approximately how many more people are less than a one hour-drive from a National Park since the motorways have been built (see **B**)?

4. What problems does increased traffic bring to National Parks?

5. How has the New Forest tried to overcome problems associated with traffic?

45

The Okehampton bypass NORTH or SOUTH?

A Statistics for Dartmoor
(© Dartmoor National Park Authority)

Number of visitors to major fee paying attractions 1989–91

	1989	1990	1991
Buckfast Abbey	551 413	552 684	535 000
Miniature Pony Centre	90 286	100 814	72 000
River Dart Country Park	64 500	60 000	53 500
Castle Drogo	109 611	110 958	112 003
Lydford Gorge	90 088	89 147	83 364

Where do tourists come from?

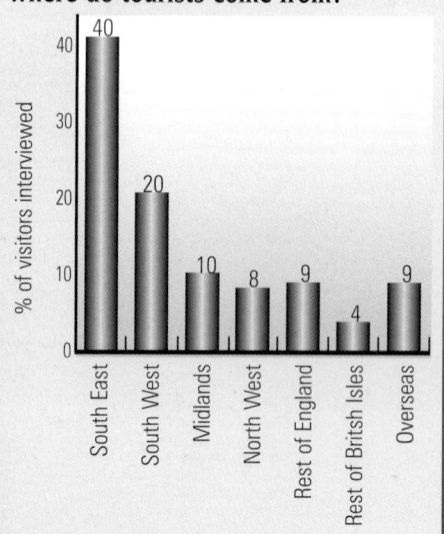

% of visitors interviewed:
- South East: 40
- South West: 20
- Midlands: 10
- North West: 8
- Rest of England: 9
- Rest of British Isles: 4
- Overseas: 9

When do visitors come to Dartmoor?

Monthly traffic movements along one of the major access roads into the Dartmoor National Park area, 1991

Figures include day visitors from home bases and tourists

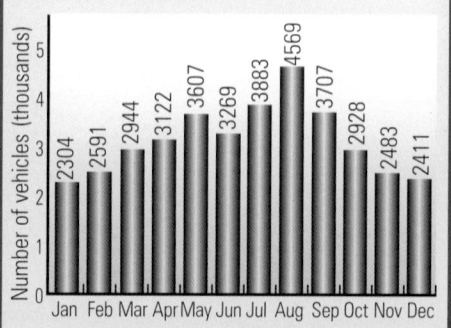

Number of vehicles (thousands):
- Jan: 2304
- Feb: 2591
- Mar: 2944
- Apr: 3122
- May: 3607
- Jun: 3269
- Jul: 3883
- Aug: 4569
- Sep: 3707
- Oct: 2928
- Nov: 2483
- Dec: 2411

Transport links are extremely important to the economic development of a region. National Parks also depend on links for accessibility to visitors and the livelihood of people who live there. Many new roads and motorways have been built to link up regions around the country. There has also been a huge increase in the amount of commercial and private vehicles on the road. Whilst the building of new roads has been necessary, it has also brought problems. Problems are particularly acute in towns and villages where many roads are old and narrow and not designed for modern traffic. The result is often congestion, pollution, danger to pedestrians and damage to buildings. The simplest solution is to build a bypass, although deciding on the line of a new road can cause further conflict.

Dartmoor National Park

Dartmoor was designated a National Park in 1951 and is characterised by its granite tors, open **moorland**, bogs, ponies and prison! At the beginning of the twentieth century tourism in the area was well established with many people visiting the moors. The number of visitors has increased and this has led to the development of **honeypot** sites, such as Buckfast Abbey, Hay Tor, Becky Falls and Lydford Gorge (**A**). The National Park is easily accessible from all directions and there are roads crossing the moors. However, the highest areas are remote and can only be visited on foot.

The Dartmoor National Park Authority is working with a number of organisations to implement a Dartmoor Area Tourism Initiative. The aims include to:

- protect and enhance the heritage of the area upon which tourism depends;
- increase the contribution made by tourism to the rural economy;
- improve the visitors' enjoyment of the area;
- reduce damage caused by tourism and ensure activities promote conservation;
- reduce visitor pressure within the park by encouraging interest in the area around the park;
- spread the economic benefits of tourism to areas around the park.

A programme of work has been set up to include the promotion of guided walks, co-ordination of events and organising public transport initiatives.

3 The Human Landscape

National Parks pp6–8
Developments in National Parks p61
Tourism pp76–84
Planning and development pp92–3

Okehampton

Okehampton is a small Devon town located to the north of the National Park boundary. It is an important centre for the surrounding farming area and is situated beneath Dartmoor's highest point, Yes Tor. Okehampton offers a number of attractions to visitors including the Museum of Dartmoor Life, Okehampton Castle, the mediaeval deer park and a wide range of specialist shops. The town is a popular base for visitors who explore the area.

The old A30 ran through Okehampton and was the main route for people travelling from London to Cornwall (**B**). Serious congestion in the town was caused by holiday traffic during peak holiday times (**A**) and by heavy goods vehicles all year round. The congestion causes safety hazards, noise, air pollution and much inconvenience to local people. There was little dispute that a bypass was needed but there was much debate as to where it should be built (**C**).

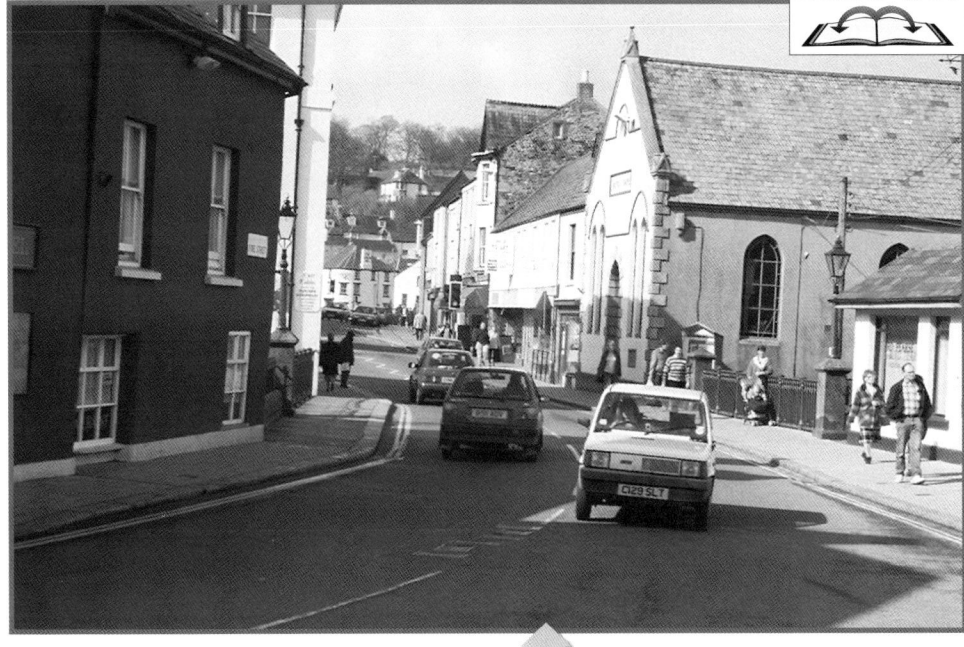

B Okehampton town centre

Key
- Okehampton
- Woodland
- – – – National Park boundary
- – · – · – Northern route
- – – – Southern route

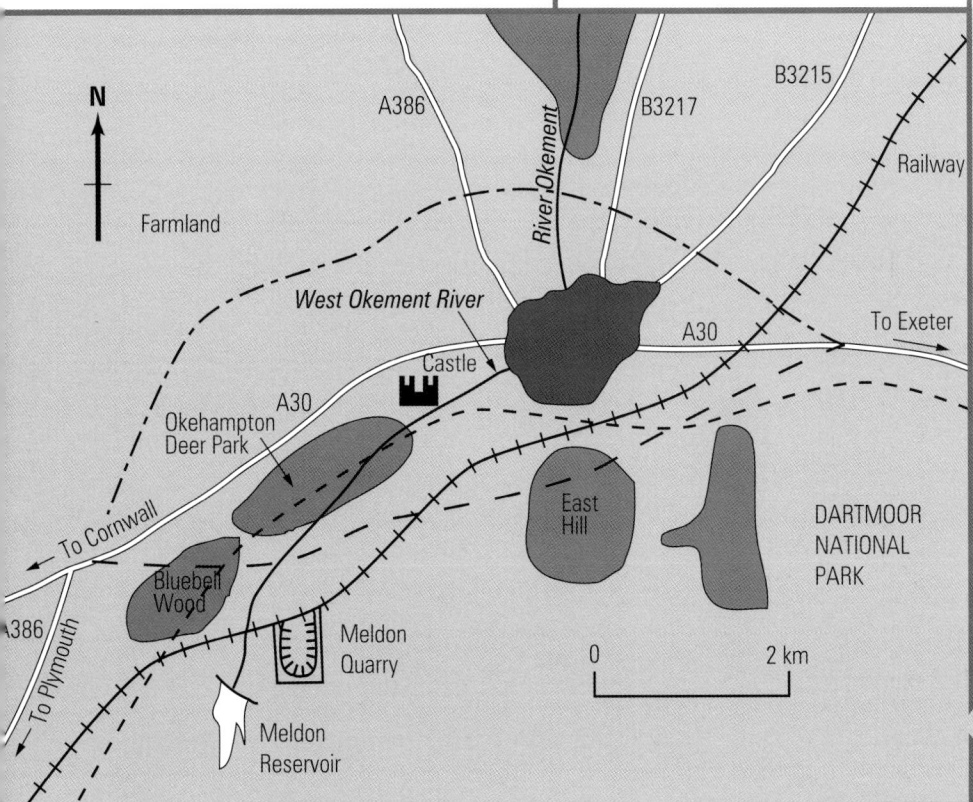

C The alternative routes for the Okehampton bypass

Activities

1. What is the main tourist attraction in the Dartmoor National Park?

2. Which are the most popular and least popular months for visitors to the Dartmoor National Park? Explain why.

3. Why do the majority of tourists come from the south?

4. Why is the Tourism Initiative in Dartmoor needed?

5. Explain why Okehampton is popular with visitors.

6. Look at **B** and explain why Okehampton town centre suffered from congestion.

47

Themes and Issues: *National Parks in the UK*

D Constructing the bypass

Length of routes
- Northern route: 10.9 kilometres
- Southern route: 8.5 kilometres

Agricultural land used (in hectares)

Agricultural land is classified on a scale of 1-5 (1 being very good, 5 being poor).

Land quality	Northern route	Southern route
3	42.0	19.5
4	24.5	18.5
5	–	13.0
Total	**66.5**	**51.0**

Slopes, poor soil and exposure mean farms to the south of Okehampton are limited to the grazing of cattle and sheep. To the north land is of a higher quality and so dairy and mixed farms are found.

Other land uses affected
- Recreation - the north of the town is seldom used for recreation as it is mainly farmland. The south has public rights of way and much open space which can be used for leisure.
- Okehampton Castle - the southern route can be seen from the castle and so spoils the mediaeval setting.
- Okehampton Deer Park - this area of woodland is protected by tree preservation orders. The park contains many important wildlife habitats.
- Bluebell Wood - this is an area of public access and is popular with local people.

Structures needed
The following is a list of features which will need to be considered in building the bypass.

	Northern route	Southern route
Rivers	1	2
Roads	5	1
Railways	1	1
Highland	0	1

A report of the National Parks policies review committee produced by the Department of the Environment in January 1976 states that:

> It is now the policy of the Government that investment in trunk roads should be directed to developing routes for long-distance traffic which should avoid National Parks; and that no new road for long-distance traffic be constructed through a National Park, or existing road upgraded unless it has been demonstrated that there is a compelling need which would not be met by any reasonable alternative means.

The White Paper 'Food From Our Own Resources' 1975, paragraph 16, and the White Paper 'Farming and the Nation' 1979, both state:

> Government policy is to ensure that wherever possible agricultural land of a higher quality is not taken for development where land of lower quality is available.

The White Paper 'Policy for Roads' 1978 states that:

> Value for money will remain an essential objective in the planning and building of roads ... where despite the best efforts of engineering design, schemes would still have a damaging effect on communities or the environment they will not be approved unless they show high economic or other benefit...

3 The Human Landscape

E Views on the bypass

Minister from the Department of Transport: I have a budget to work to and want the best value for money.

Member of the Archaeological Society: There are many sites of interest which are still being investigated in the northern parts of the National Park.

Employee of Dartmoor National Park: The government has said that no new roads should be built through National Parks, especially when there is an alternative.

Resident of Brightley Road: I moved to the north of the town five years ago for the peace and quiet. This is now under threat.

A 95 day public inquiry was held to hear the proposals and arguments for and against the two routes. In August 1986 the Department of the Environment announced its preferred route south of Okehampton and through the National Park. The bypass took 104 weeks to build and cost £16.6 million. The road was officially opened on 19 July 1988 (**F**).

BYPASS OPENING ENDS DECADES OF ARGUMENT

Decades of conflict and argument which have dominated the life and thought of Okehampton came to a final end just before Christmas with the opening of the second carriageway of the bypass.

For the first time since the days of the Saxons Okehampton town no longer lies across the main route from the rest of Britain to Cornwall.

(© *Okehampton Times*, 1988)

Activities

1 Do you think the following people would support the northern or the southern route? Explain your answer.
- member of the Ramblers Association;
- farmer who lives to the north of the town;
- member of the Road Haulage Association;
- employee of the Devon Tourist Board?

2 Using all the information in this section explain why the southern route was chosen?

Looking west along Okehampton bypass **F**

49

THEMES AND ISSUES: **National Parks in the UK**

Decision making exercise

Whitton is a busy market town on the edge of a National Park. The town receives visitors from around the country. It provides an ideal stopping off point as it acts as a 'gateway' to the mountains. The town is also at the junction of several main roads serving the region. Oxbury Construction Company has been awarded the contract to build a bypass around Whitton. This will reduce the congestion in the town's narrow streets.

Imagine you are one of the company's consultants and have been given the responsibility of assessing the cost and environmental impact of building the bypass. There are three possible routes which are to be considered (**G**).

Remember: In this activity you will need to think about and discuss some of the issues which arise in National Parks. Consider the information from the case study of the Okehampton bypass.

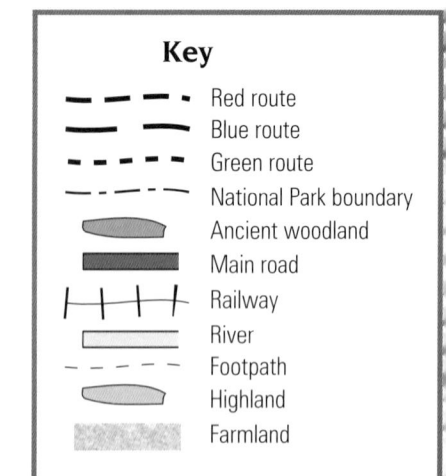

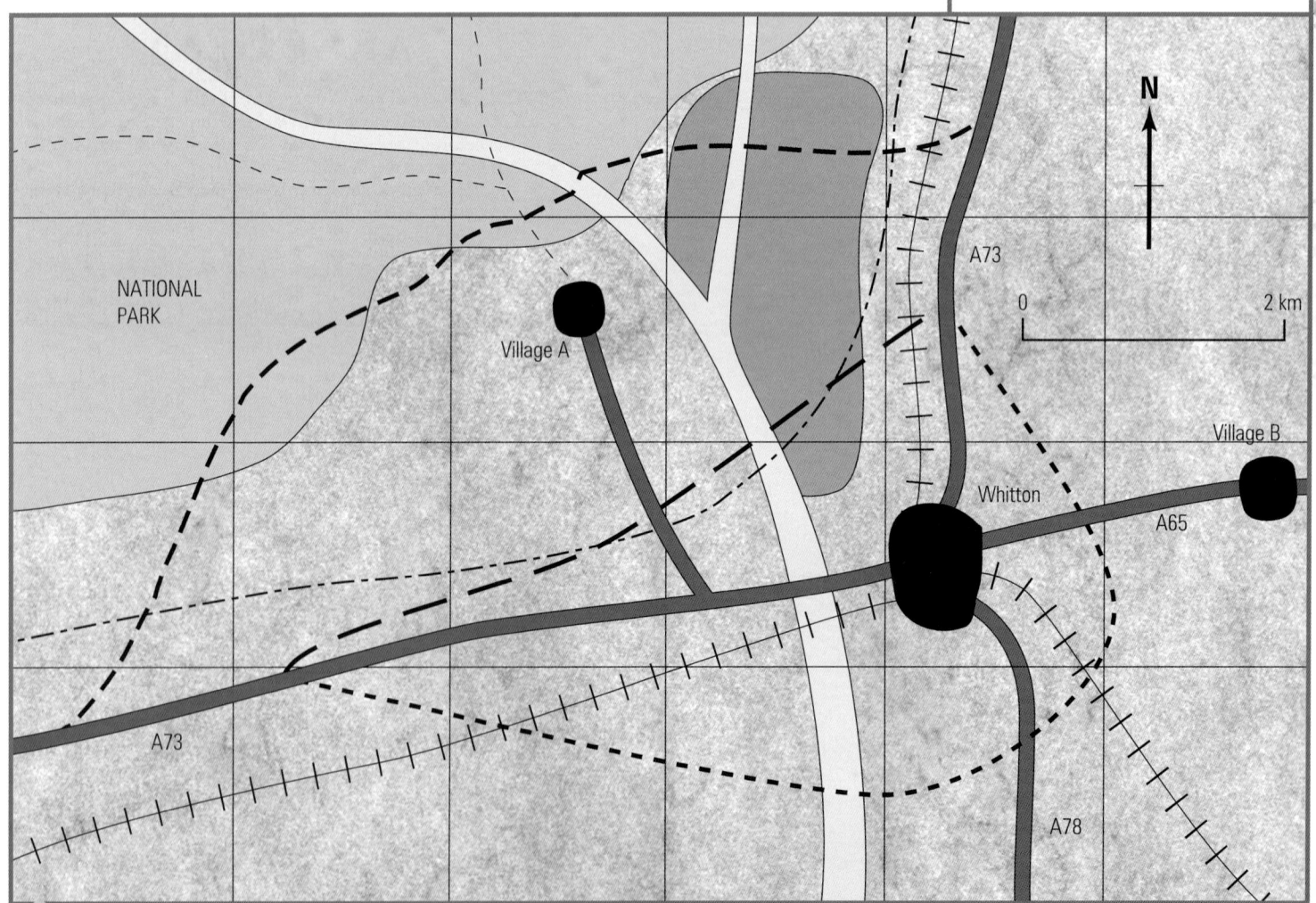

Key
- Red route
- Blue route
- Green route
- National Park boundary
- Ancient woodland
- Main road
- Railway
- River
- Footpath
- Highland
- Farmland

G A bypass around Whitton?

50

3 The Human Landscape

Current costing for construction	£ million
Basic cost per km	1.0
Additional costs:	
Crossing a major road	0.5
Crossing a railway line	0.5
Cutting through highland	0.5
Crossing a river	0.5

Agricultural farmland (hectares)

Land quality	Red route	Blue route	Green route
2	-	-	10.5
3	10	23	38
4	37.5	19.5	25.5
5	22.5	13.5	-
Total	70	56	74

The figures refer to the amount and quality of the farmland each route would take up (2 being the highest quality of land)

You must submit a report which should include the following information:

1. Calculate the economic cost of the three routes, remembering to take into account not only the basic cost per kilometre but also the additional structures needed. To do this copy and complete the table below. *(6 marks)*

Route	Distance in km.	Basic cost	Crossings			Through highland	TOTAL COST
			Road	River	Railway		
Red							

2. Why is the cost to the environment more difficult to measure? Discuss what some of these costs could be. *(6 marks)*

Extension
Devise a method to assess the environmental cost. For example, you might want to use a scoring system in which you could take two points off a score for every kilometre through a National Park.

3. Decide which route you would choose and explain your decision. You should consider the need to protect the National Park, the people living in the area and the possible effects on visitors. *(8 marks)*

To make your report look more professional you may want to use a word processor to present your work.

4 ECONOMIC ACTIVITIES

National Parks are often seen primarily as a place for recreation. However, they are the location for all types of industry from farming and quarrying (primary industry) to manufacturing (secondary) and services (tertiary). The inhabitants of these areas depend on such industry for their livelihood. National Parks should therefore be viewed as a working environment in which recreation can take place.

Hill sheep farming

Agriculture plays an important role in the development of the National Parks' landscape.

Sheep farming is the main agricultural land use in the Lake District. A large proportion of the park is mountainous which leads to harsh environmental conditions:

- Steep slopes make the use of machinery difficult and produce thin acidic soils that will only support a limited vegetation.
- Temperatures tend to be cool in summer due to the altitude (with every 1000 metre increase in altitude temperatures decrease by six degrees Celsius) which gives a shorter growing season. Winters are mild due to the warming effects of the **North Atlantic Drift**.
- Rainfall is high throughout the year. The increased cloud cover reduces the amount of sunshine hours and the rainfall leaches the nutrients out of the thin soils.

These factors make the land unsuitable for arable farming. In the central areas of the Lake District hill sheep farming dominates, whilst in the valleys and on the fringes of the park dairy farming can be found. Due to the poorer quality of the land people need to farm a wider area to make it viable. Sheep farming can be described as **extensive** and **commercial**.

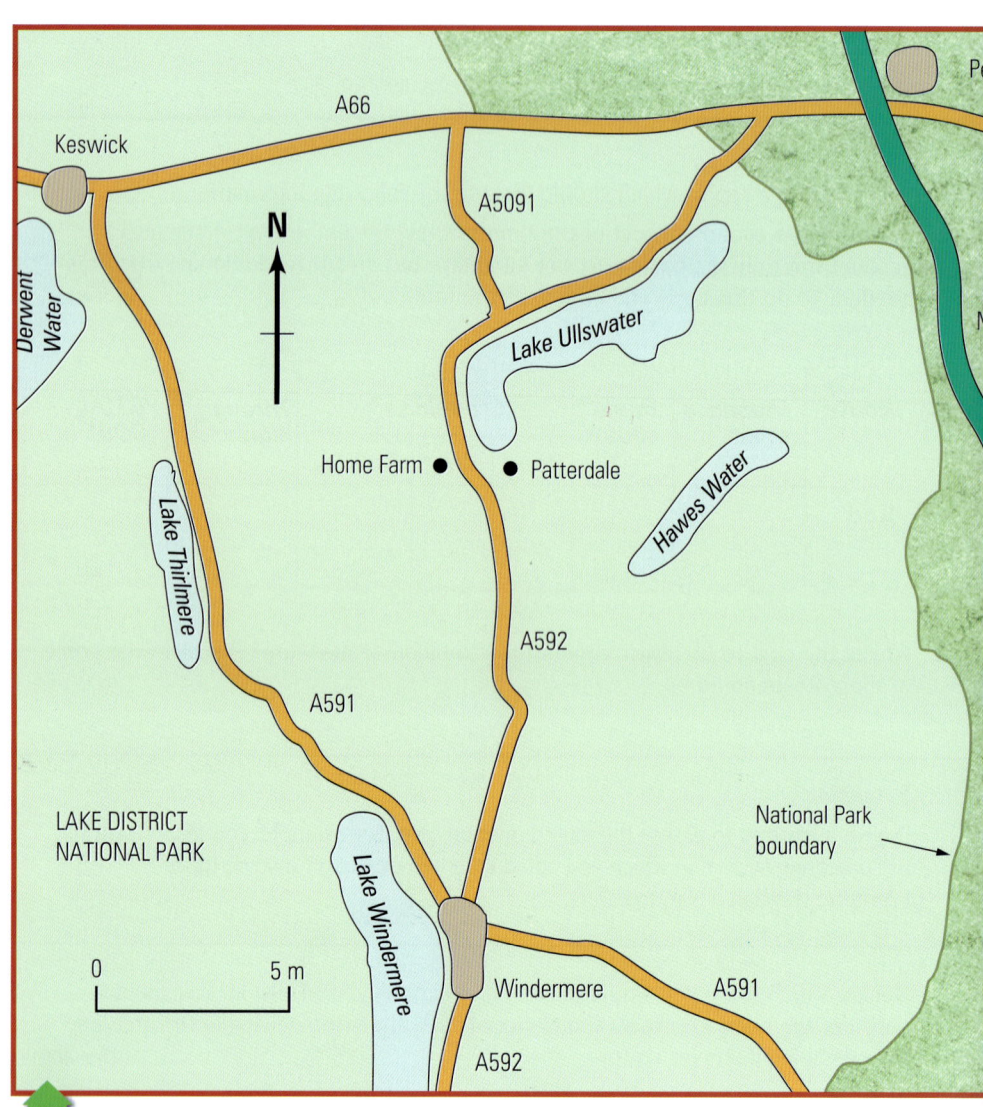

A Location of Home Farm

Home Farm, Patterdale, Lake District

Home Farm is located at the southern end of Lake Ullswater near Patterdale in the Lake District (**A**). The farm is owned by Mr and Mrs Beaty who have worked there for 21 years. It is a pastoral farm concentrating mainly on sheep. However, some cattle are kept.

B Home Farm

4 Economic Activities

National Parks pp6–9
Nant Ffrancon p13
Farming in Exmoor p90

D Profile of Home Farm

Location	Patterdale, Ullswater valley, Lake District (20 km SW of Penrith)
Size	277 ha in total (65 ha of which was bought recently to produce more hay and silage)
Owners	Mr and Mrs Beaty own 142 ha and a further 85 ha are rented from the Patterdale Hall Estate
Labour	one full time plus casual workers (depending on the season)
Animals	sheep - 350 Herdwick, 600 Swaledale, 300 Cheviots
	32 suckler cows (this is to breed calves for sale at the meat market)
	five sheep dogs
Crops	hay and silage to feed animals
Machinery	two four-wheel drive tractors, a motorbike and trailer, two vans, clipping machines, baling machinery, mower and assorted trailers
Market	sheep and cows for market at Penrith
	a range of products from the sheep

The physical geography of Home Farm

Altitude	150-400 m
Temperature	mean July temperature - 13.8°C
	mean January temperature - 2.5°C
Precipitation	mean annual rainfall - 1914 mm
Growing season	May to September
Type of soil	in valley bottom **gley soils** (prone to waterlogging) and on the fell sides thin acidic **brown earth soils**

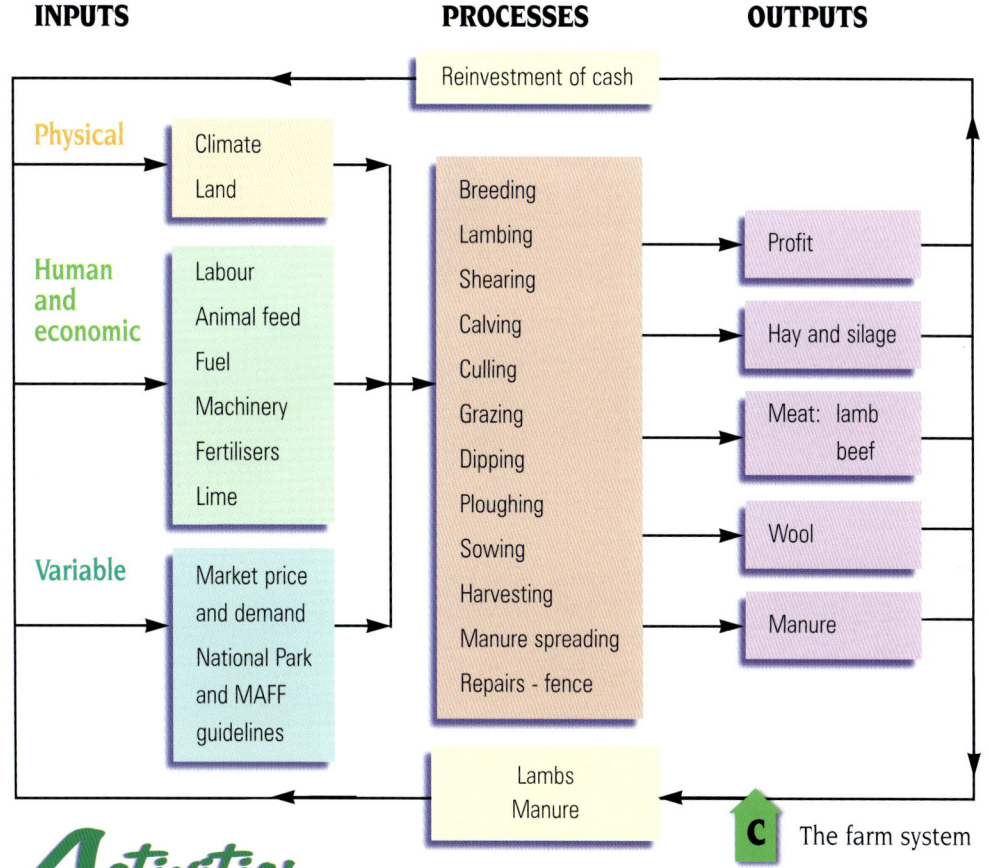

INPUTS

Physical
- Climate
- Land

Human and economic
- Labour
- Animal feed
- Fuel
- Machinery
- Fertilisers
- Lime

Variable
- Market price and demand
- National Park and MAFF guidelines

PROCESSES

Reinvestment of cash

- Breeding
- Lambing
- Shearing
- Calving
- Culling
- Grazing
- Dipping
- Ploughing
- Sowing
- Harvesting
- Manure spreading
- Repairs - fence

Lambs
Manure

OUTPUTS

- Profit
- Hay and silage
- Meat: lamb, beef
- Wool
- Manure

C The farm system

Activities

1 What is meant by the following terms:
  a extensive farming;
  b commercial farming;
  c pastoral farming?

2 Sheep farming is often the only option in upland areas. Explain why this natural environment is suitable for this type of farming.

3 Using **A** and **B** describe the location and site of Home Farm.

4 What are the main inputs to the farm (see **C**)? What problems might the farmer face if one of these inputs is more or less than the normal amount?

53

THEMES AND ISSUES: *National Parks in the UK*

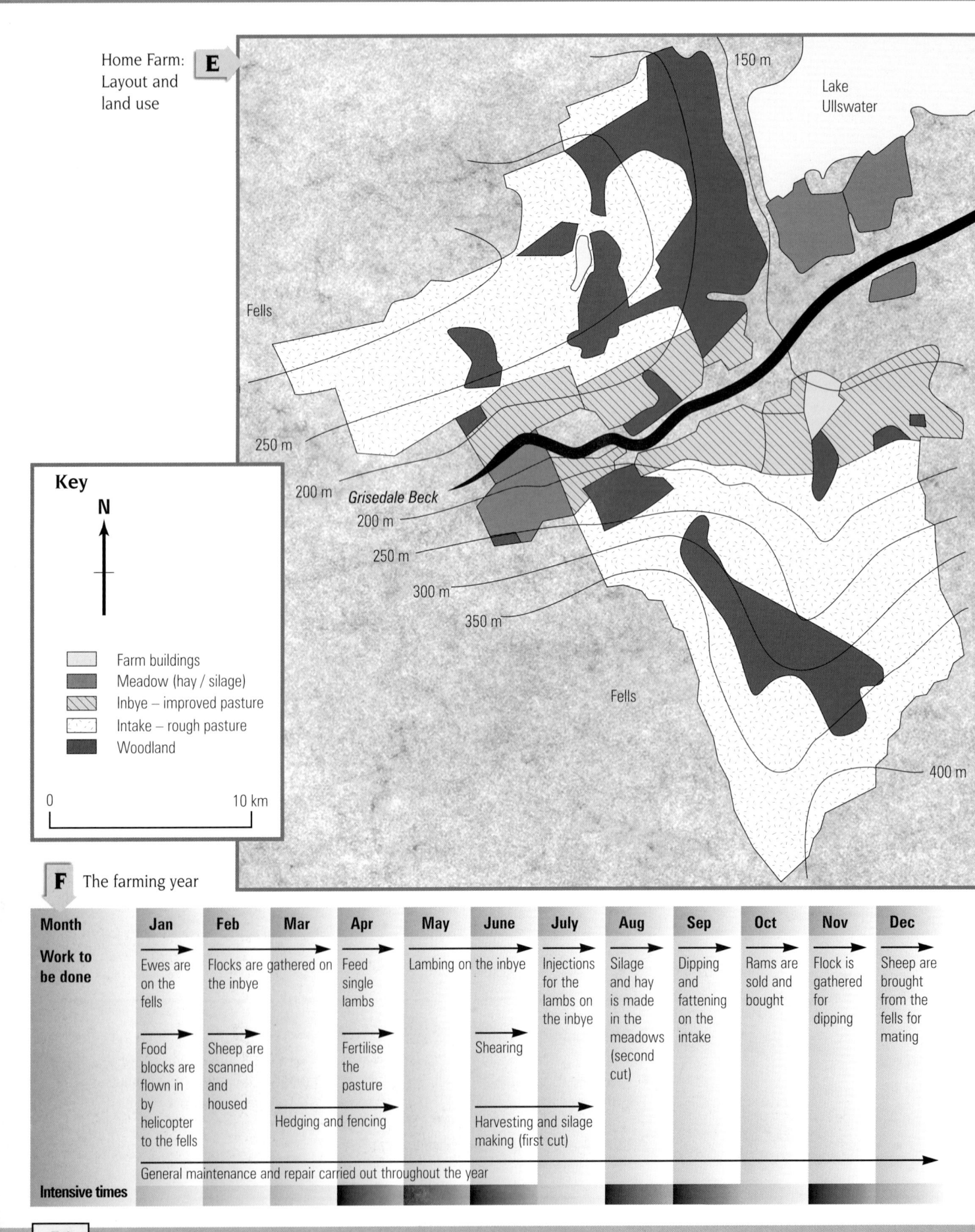

E Home Farm: Layout and land use

Key

- Farm buildings
- Meadow (hay / silage)
- Inbye – improved pasture
- Intake – rough pasture
- Woodland

0 — 10 km

Lake Ullswater

Fells

Grisedale Beck

Fells

150 m, 200 m, 250 m, 200 m, 250 m, 300 m, 350 m, 400 m

F The farming year

Month	Jan	Feb	Mar	Apr	May	June	July	Aug	Sep	Oct	Nov	Dec
Work to be done	Ewes are on the fells	Flocks are gathered on the inbye		Feed single lambs	Lambing on the inbye		Injections for the lambs on the inbye	Silage and hay is made in the meadows (second cut)	Dipping and fattening on the intake	Rams are sold and bought	Flock is gathered for dipping	Sheep are brought from the fells for mating
	Food blocks are flown in by helicopter to the fells	Sheep are scanned and housed		Fertilise the pasture		Shearing						
			Hedging and fencing →				Harvesting and silage making (first cut) →					
	General maintenance and repair carried out throughout the year →											

Intensive times

54

4 Economic Activities

Land use

To get the most out of the land the farmer has made a series of decisions as to what the land is to be used for (**E**). The farm buildings are located on the valley floor for easy access to and from the farm. The land surrounding the farm buildings is known as the inbye. This is improved pasture which is only used at certain times of the year (see **F**). The soil here is thicker and of a higher quality producing good pasture, although it has a tendency to become waterlogged. This land is used for the more labour intensive tasks and so its proximity to the farm buildings saves the farmer a great deal of time. The steeper slopes surrounding the farm are used for rough pasture and woodland (the intake). The farm has **fell rights** on the sides of Helvellyn mountain and Thornhow fells where the sheep are kept for most of the year.

Diversification

Many farmers have felt a need to **diversify** their activities to bring in an additional income. Several years ago Home Farm converted part of the farmhouse to offer bed and breakfast to people walking the 'Coast to Coast' path (a long-distance footpath going across the width of Northern England). The Beatys also offer tours of their farm to give visitors knowledge and experience of different farming activities.

Recent changes

In 1987 The Ministry of Agriculture, Fisheries and Food (MAFF) introduced the **Environmentally Sensitive Areas** (ESA) scheme. This scheme aimed to protect and enhance landscapes of national importance from the effects of intensive use. Farmers who enter into this scheme are offered payments by MAFF to carry out these agricultural practices.

Three years ago Mr and Mrs Beaty entered into an ESA agreement with MAFF. In the agreement the farm receives payments to reduce the number of sheep on the fells to try and stop overgrazing. The stock has been reduced by one-third to 1250. Under the ESA agreement the farm is restricted in its activities and animals it can farm. Also, alterations to the layout of any part of the farm must first receive permission from MAFF.

Activities

1. Using the information in this section describe and explain the land use of Home Farm.

2. Why have some farmers attempted to diversify their activities?

3. **a** Diagram **G** shows a sketch of a typical hill farm. Copy the diagram and label the following land uses:
   - fell;
   - farm buildings;
   - meadow;
   - intake;
   - inbye.

   b What activities take place in the different parts of the farm you have labelled?

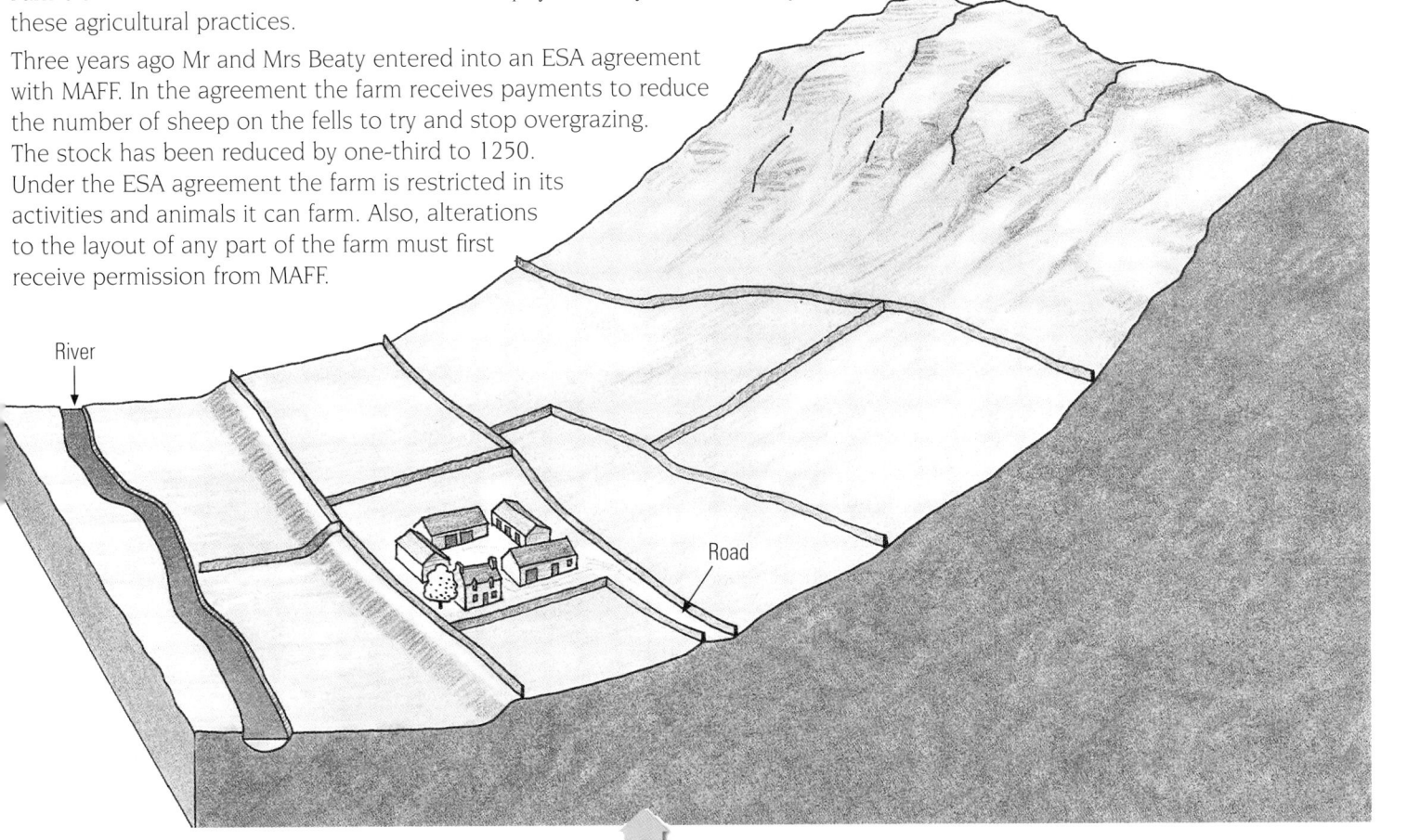

G Sketch of a typical hill farm

THEMES AND ISSUES: *National Parks in the UK*

Interactions

Industries do not exist in isolation as many links are formed between them. Tourism in National Parks is a major industry and brings in a large amount of money to the local economy. Farmers have cashed in on tourists by providing bed and breakfast, tours of the farm and camping areas. A new trend that has become popular with both farmers and tourists is the development of camping barns (**H** and **I**).

Runnage, Postbridge

This barn, in the middle of the Moor close to Bellever Forest and the River Dart, sleeps 15 and has a camping field alongside for bigger groups.
A big farmhouse breakfast is also available. Toilets and showers are within the barn.

H An advert for a camping barn

DARTMOOR AND EXMOOR CAMPING BARN NETWORK

NOT many people have heard of camping barns - or stone tents as they are nicknamed - but they are not really a new concept.

Youth hostels began as very simple accommodation for hikers and bikers, often looked after by part-time volunteers or wardens.

Camping barns, like many of these original hostels, provide simple accommodation with a communal sleeping area, a self-catering area, toilets and running water. Some will also provide showers, heating, drying facilities and meals for those who need their comfort! They are looked after by the farmer who is on site anyway so there is no need for a paid warden.

The YHA believes that there is a market for small, simple accommodation and has been involved in setting up camping barns along with the Countryside Commission, National Parks and Devon County Council.

The YHA provides marketing and a booking office for the individual farmers who own the barns. Other support has included finding grant aid from the Rural Development Commission and the European Union to help with renovations.

In an attempt to encourage more people to leave their cars behind and strike out on foot, the YHA is working with the National Parks and Devon County Council to set up walking routes and maybe cycling routes between barns.

I Newspaper article on camping barns
(Adapted from article in the Dartmoor Visitor, 1995)

An aerial view of Runnage Farm

Runnage Farm

Runnage Farm is located in Dartmoor National Park and is managed by the Coaker family. They have a tenancy agreement with the **Duchy of Cornwall** to farm the land to produce sheep and cattle for meat. Animals are carefully selected for productivity and ability to cope with the harsh conditions on Dartmoor.

The farm consists of a number of buildings centred around the traditionally built farmstead (**K**). As the farm has developed, new purpose-built outhouses have been added to accommodate the sheep and cows. The farm also has rights to graze livestock (up to a certain amount) on the common land around the area.

The farm has **diversified** offering certain recreational facilities to tourists. One of the fields in the inbye area has become a camping site, whilst one of the old traditional buildings has been converted into a camping barn (**J**). This is a basic building, able to accommodate 15 people. It provides a sleeping area and washing facilities. This enterprise has been going for three years and has proved to be reasonably successful. An extension to this facility is now being considered to provide a bunkhouse for larger groups.

4 Economic Activities

J A plan of the farm buildings, Runnage Farm

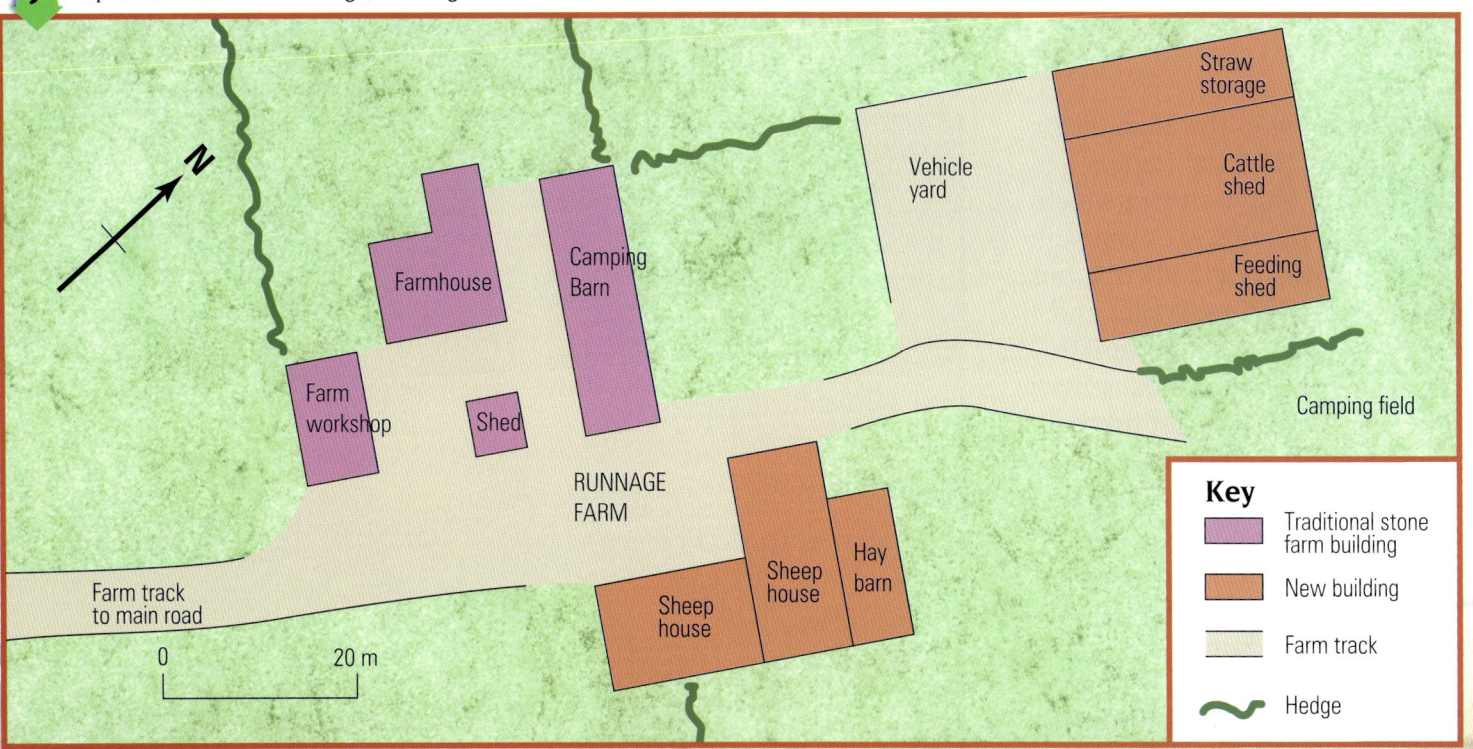

Key
- Traditional stone farm building
- New building
- Farm track
- Hedge

Buildings labelled on plan: Straw storage, Cattle shed, Feeding shed, Vehicle yard, Farmhouse, Camping Barn, Farm workshop, Shed, RUNNAGE FARM, Sheep house, Sheep house, Hay barn, Camping field, Farm track to main road.

Scale: 0 — 20 m

Activities

1. What are the advantages of the camping barns to:
   a the farmer;
   b the camper?

2. What are the disadvantages of an increased number of camping barns in National Parks?

3. Design an advert to promote the use of camping barns in National Parks. Use a word processor, if possible, to present the work.

4. Study the plan and photograph of Runnage Farm and answer the following questions:
   a Describe the camping barn (mention where it is and what it is like).
   b Why is it important to have the sheep in buildings close to the farmhouse at certain times of the year?
   c Explain why the inbye is located behind the farm buildings.

57

Quarrying in the

Quarrying in the Yorkshire Dales National Park is a traditional industry which dates back hundreds of years. The stone was originally dug out by hand at small local pits and used to build the characteristic dry stone walls and houses. As National Parks were set up to protect the countryside, quarrying is often viewed as a major source of conflict by outsiders. Quarries can be noisy, dusty and unsightly. They have, however, been part of the landscape since long before National Parks were established and provide important local employment opportunities. The quarry owners and managers have to work with the National Park Authority to make this industry as environmentally sound as possible.

A Limestone is a valuable resource – examples of its use

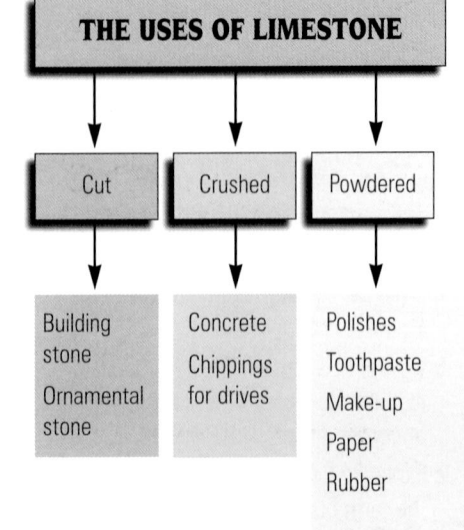

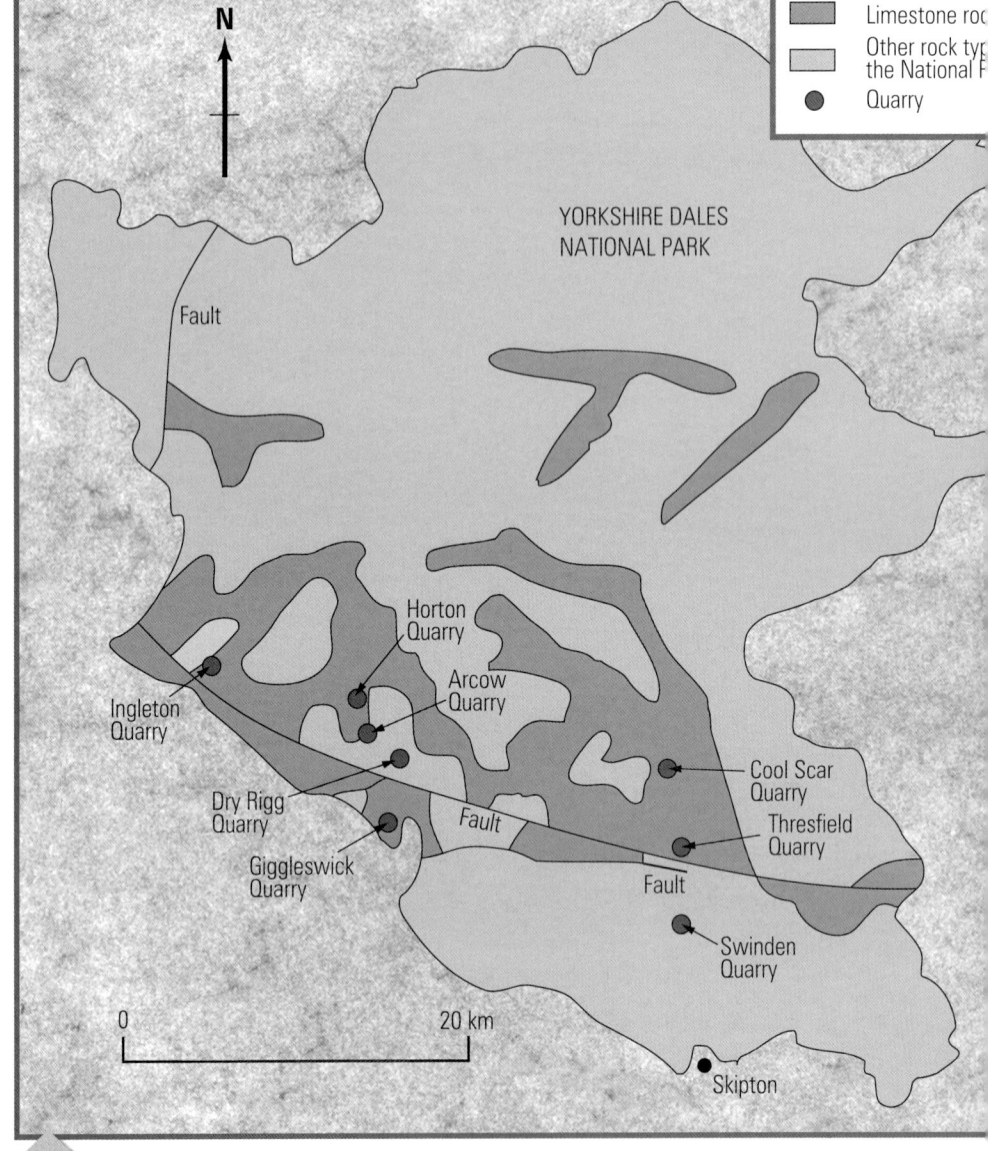

THE USES OF LIMESTONE

- Cut
  - Building stone
  - Ornamental stone
- Crushed
  - Concrete
  - Chippings for drives
- Powdered
  - Polishes
  - Toothpaste
  - Make-up
  - Paper
  - Rubber
  - Paints and plastics
  - Resins
  - Bleach
  - Glass
  - Tanning
  - Sewage beds
  - Water purification
  - Cement
  - Cement blocks
  - Fertilisers
  - Animal feed
  - Removal of sulphur dioxide (SO_2)
  - Ore smelting

B The distribution of limestone and quarries in the Yorkshire Dales

The uses of limestone

Limestone is one of the most widely used raw materials. Its many different uses include the manufacture of products such as glass, toothpaste and fertilisers (**A**). As the rock takes millions of years to form it is classed as a finite, or non-renewable resource.

58

Yorkshire Dales

4 Economic Activities

National Parks pp6–8
Limestone pp22–3
Planning and development pp92–3

Swinden Quarry

Swinden Quarry is one of the largest quarries in north Yorkshire, covering 61 hectares of land and producing 20 per cent of the limestone in this area. It is located one kilometre north of Cracoe village on the B6265 in the Yorkshire Dales National Park (**C**). It is one of eight limestone quarries in the park (**B**). Swinden Quarry dates back to the turn of the century when traditional labour intensive methods were used. Today the quarry, owned by Tilcon Limited, is fully mechanised and operates on a much larger scale (**D** and **E**). The quarry employs 80 people, the majority of whom are local, and extracts approximately 2 million tonnes of limestone a year (**F**). Swinden Quarry has a worldwide market.

C The location of Swinden Quarry

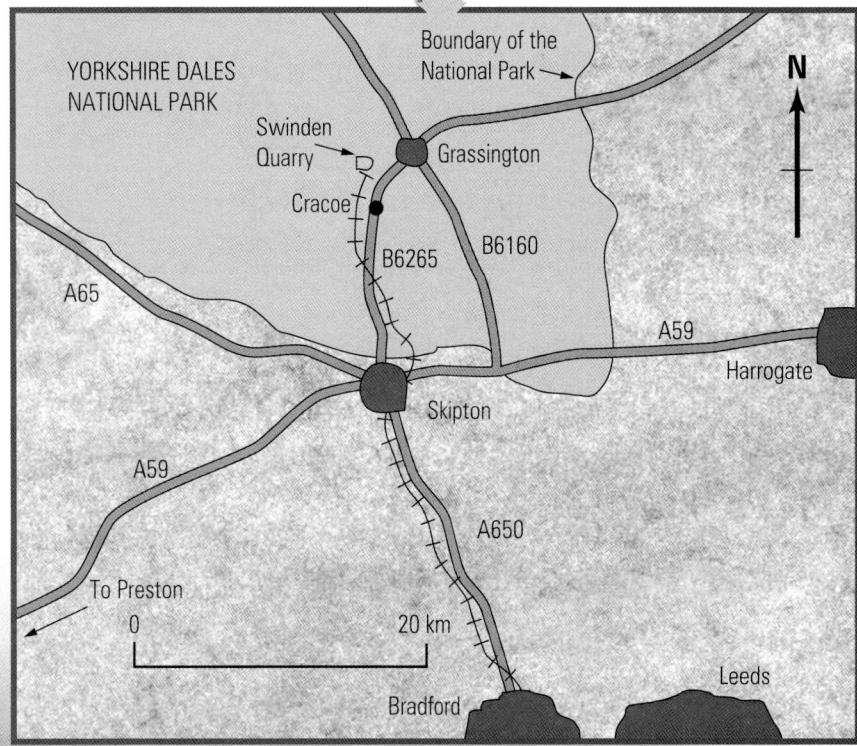

D Swinden Quarry

E Inside Swinden Quarry

F Total sales of limestone from Swinden Quarry

Activities

1. List five uses of limestone in and around your home.

2. Describe the distribution of limestone quarries in the Yorkshire Dales. Try to explain this distribution.

3. Using the photograph of inside Swinden Quarry (**E**) draw a sketch of the quarry and label the following features: stock piles, rock face, quarry floor, water pools, JCB digger.

Themes and Issues: *National Parks in the UK*

How the quarry works

- Extraction - two drill rigs (**G**) operate at the rock face and create holes into which explosives are inserted. Each blast brings down 35 000 tonnes of rock. This rock is then transferred to the crushers by truck.
- Crushing - three crushers reduce the rock in size.
- Screening - the rock is sorted into seven different sizes by passing it over meshes. This is then stored in bins or stock piles (see **E** on page 59).
- Blending - different rock sizes are mixed together to meet the requirements of the customer.
- Lime production - limestone is dropped into the kilns and heated to 1200 degrees Celsius. This turns the calcium carbonate into calcium oxide which is used for the production of many chemicals.

G A drill rig at work

- Manufacture of cement blocks (bricks) - the crushed limestone can be compressed with cement and water into building blocks which can vary in size depending on requirements. Each year 2.5 to 3 million blocks are produced and are in great demand.
- Distribution - Swinden Quarry has a railway line that links the site to the main line at Skipton. Due to the heavy loads it also has its own engine to help shunt the trucks out. The majority of the products are distributed by road. Quarry vehicles are continuously sprayed with water to clean the wheels. All road and rail trucks are covered before leaving the quarry.

4 Economic Activities

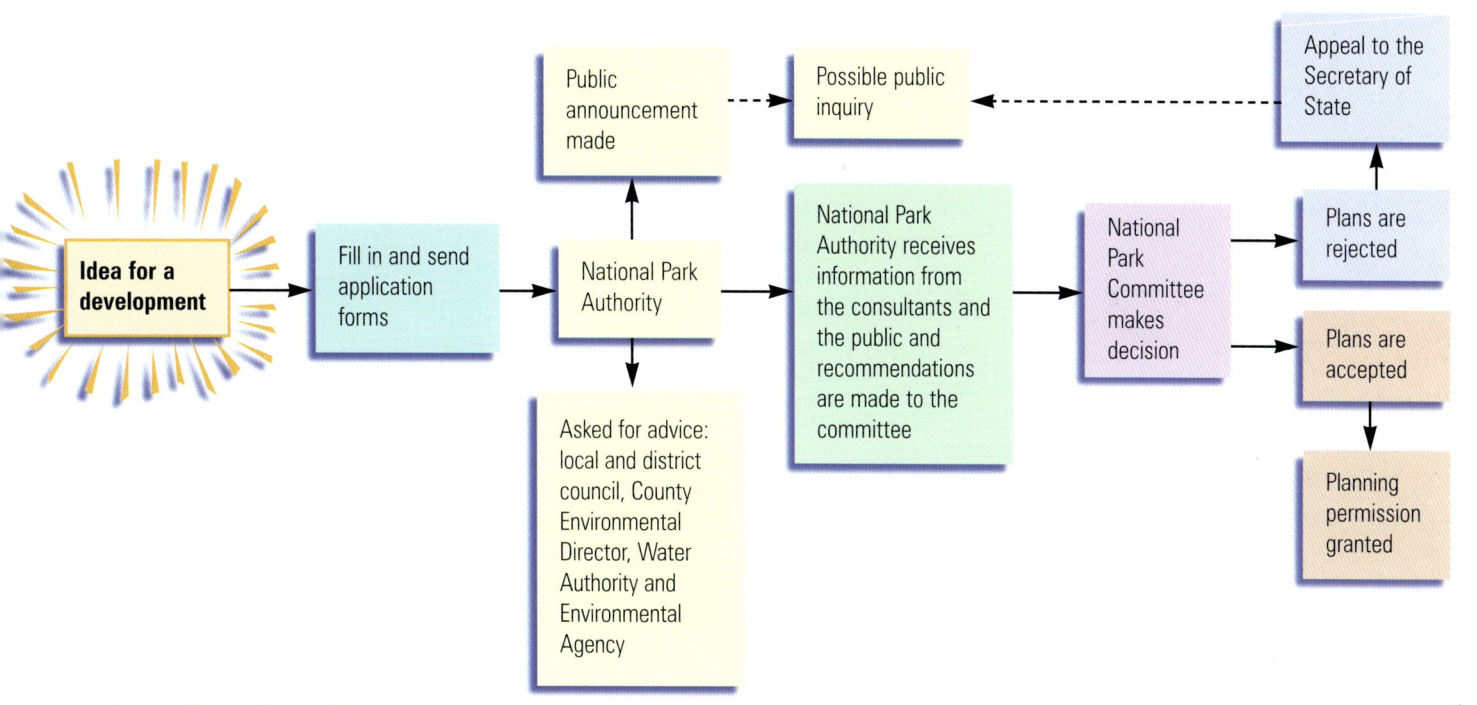

H Developments in National Parks - the planning procedure

Flow chart:
- Idea for a development → Fill in and send application forms → National Park Authority
- National Park Authority → Public announcement made ⇢ Possible public inquiry
- National Park Authority → Asked for advice: local and district council, County Environmental Director, Water Authority and Environmental Agency
- → National Park Authority receives information from the consultants and the public and recommendations are made to the committee → National Park Committee makes decision
- → Plans are rejected → Appeal to the Secretary of State ⇢ Possible public inquiry
- → Plans are accepted → Planning permission granted

Extension plans for the quarry

Tilcon had permission to quarry until the year 2048 but were only allowed to extract a further 12 million tonnes of limestone. As the quality of the limestone is good and there is still much remaining in the ground, Tilcon applied for permission to extend the quarry both outwards and downwards. In October 1993 the planning application (**H**) was put in which outlined plans for a new crushing and screening plant as well as the expansion of the quarry itself. In February 1994, after the case had been to a public inquiry, the application was refused due to the increasing impact the quarry would have had on the National Park.

In December 1994 a revised application was submitted which received planning approval. This allowed the quarry to extend downwards by a further 100 metres and to build a new crushing and screening plant inside the quarry. This will enable Tilcon to quarry a further 40 million tonnes of rock until the year 2020 when the quarry will be finished. Several conditions were agreed upon and they include:

- Road haulage is restricted to 1.5 million tonnes per year and quarry traffic is restricted to certain times of the week.
- Operation times are between 6 am and 10 pm Monday to Saturday in an attempt to reduce noise.
- The sides of Swinden Hill are to remain in place and the area is to be landscaped.
- After 2020 the quarry will be reclaimed and used as a nature conservation area with a deep central lake.

Exam practice

1. What is a finite resource? *(2 marks)*

2. Why is limestone such a valuable resource? *(2 marks)*

3. Suggest reasons why quarry output has increased (see **F**). *(2 marks)*

4. How has human activity affected the beauty of the Yorkshire Dales National Park? *(6 marks)*

5. The Yorkshire Dales is an area where there are conflicting demands on the environment. With reference to Swinden Quarry describe the problems which arise from such conflicts. Suggest how Tilcon and the National Park Authority have attempted to reduce the impact of the quarry on the surrounding countryside. *(8 marks)*

THEMES AND ISSUES: **National Parks in the UK**

Public inquiry

When a quarry closes, it is the responsibility of the company who owns the site to restore the land to its former state or find an alternative use for the area. The quarry owners, the National Park Authority and the local council decide how the land should be used. The quarry company has responsibility for the area for several years after the site is closed. A decision is reached based on social and economic factors.

Background

A limestone quarry located within a National Park (**I**) has been extracting rock for over 40 years. The quarry is due to close in four years' time. When a quarry closes a number of schemes for restoration are available (**J**). A public meeting has been called to discuss the options and to make recommendations to the National Park Authority who will then make the final decision.

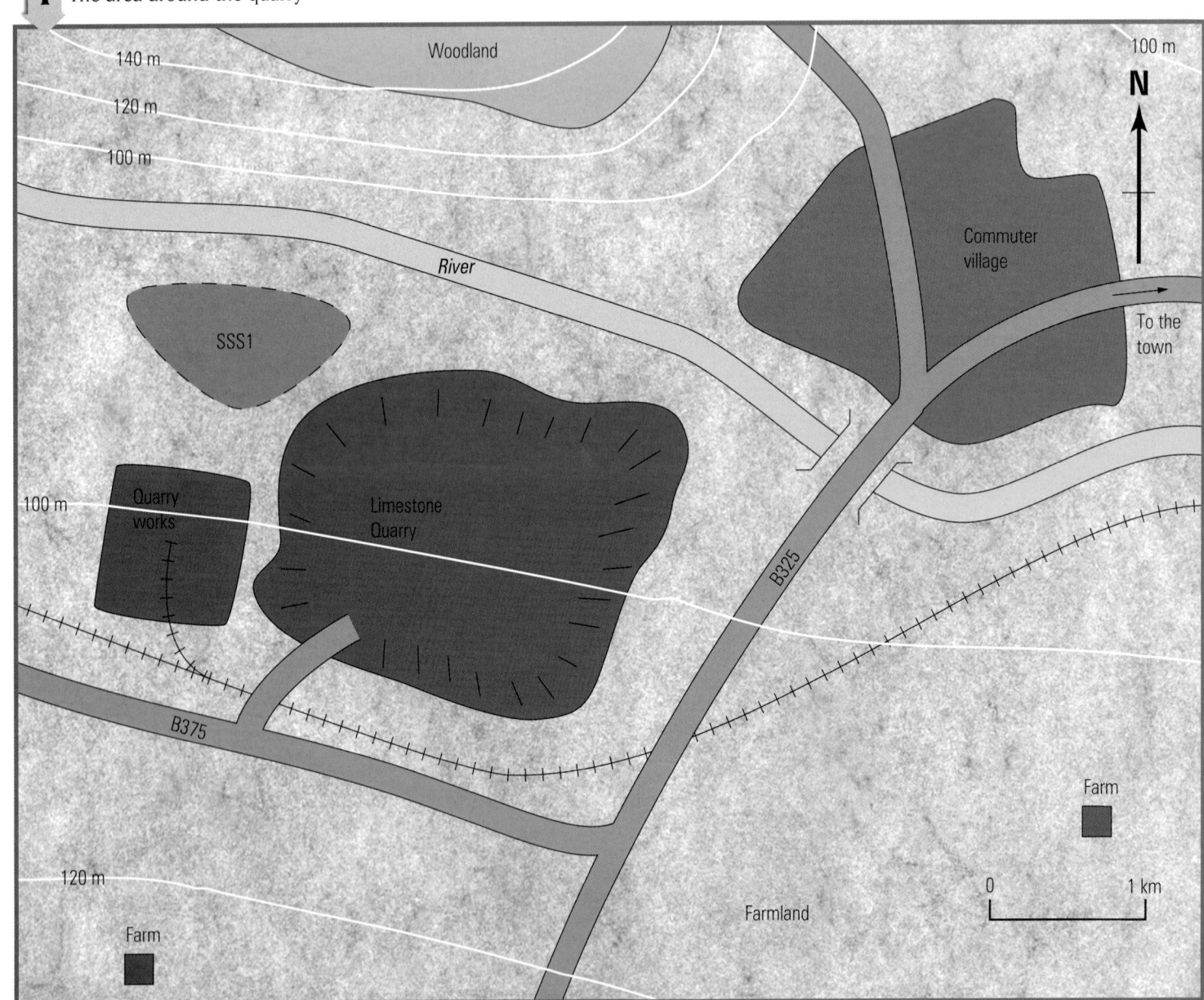

I The area around the quarry

4 Economic Activities

J The restoration options available

- **Landfill** - waste disposal is a very important issue as the UK is running out of storage space for waste. The quarry could be used for landfill which, once completed, could then be converted to farmland or playing fields. The quarry would have to be lined before filling began to stop pollution escaping into waterways. Whilst this is an economical way of using the land, social and environmental problems may arise. Methane gas is given off when material decomposes, which can be explosive. This plan would also mean the high levels of traffic would continue.

- **Building** - the local village has become very popular with commuters and housing is in great demand. Building houses would create local employment and the increased number of people may contribute to the local economy. However, this development would take many years to complete as the filling material would need time to settle to prevent subsidence (sinking or settling of the ground). Consideration also needs to be given to the effect of more residents in the National Park.

- **Leisure** - the quarry could be flooded and the surrounding area landscaped to provide water sports facilities. This would create permanent jobs and would bring money into the local economy. The area could be used for a number of sports such as sailing, windsurfing and canoeing as well as fishing.

- **Farmland** - the quarry could be returned to agricultural use. The quarrying often improves the drainage of the area and if there is suitable infill material available the land could be highly productive. This would merge with the surrounding farming landscape. This option would not create long-term employment for many people.

- **Nature reserve** - the quarry could be partly infilled to provide an area for water and wildlife habitats could be created on land. With careful planning a rich diversity of flora and fauna could be established. This area could provide an important site of interest both locally and regionally.

Role play and tasks

1. Work in groups of six. Five people should each take on one of the following roles:
   - a local builder;
   - a farmer who lives close to the quarry;
   - the quarry manager;
   - a member of Britain's Wildlife Trust;
   - a representative of the English Tourist Board.

   Using the information provided you are to decide which restoration scheme you would be in favour of and the reasons why. Then take it in turns to give a short speech about which option you prefer and why. This can be done in the setting of a public meeting.

   The sixth person should take on the role of the chairperson, who will be in charge of the meeting. When each person has given their views time should be allowed for questions and discussion (you must remain in your role).

2. As a group you are now to assume the role of members of the committee of the National Park Authority. You have the task of deciding which scheme is best suited to the site. Further discussion will be necessary before a final decision is reached. Use the proposals and discussion from the public meeting to help you make your decision.

3. You must now write a short report which includes the following information:
   - the possible options for the site (this should include arguments put forward by the people at the meeting in task 1);
   - the option chosen by the committee;
   - the reasons why that option was chosen.

Exam practice

1. What needs to be done to restore the land after a quarry has been closed? *(2 marks)*

2. What opportunities can be created by restoring areas which have been quarried? *(4 marks)*

Texaco in Pembrokeshire

Crude oil is of little use in the form in which it is extracted from the earth. But it is the raw material for many products from chemicals to polishes and tar to fuel. The refining of oil which leads to the manufacture of these products is an example of a secondary industry (**B**).

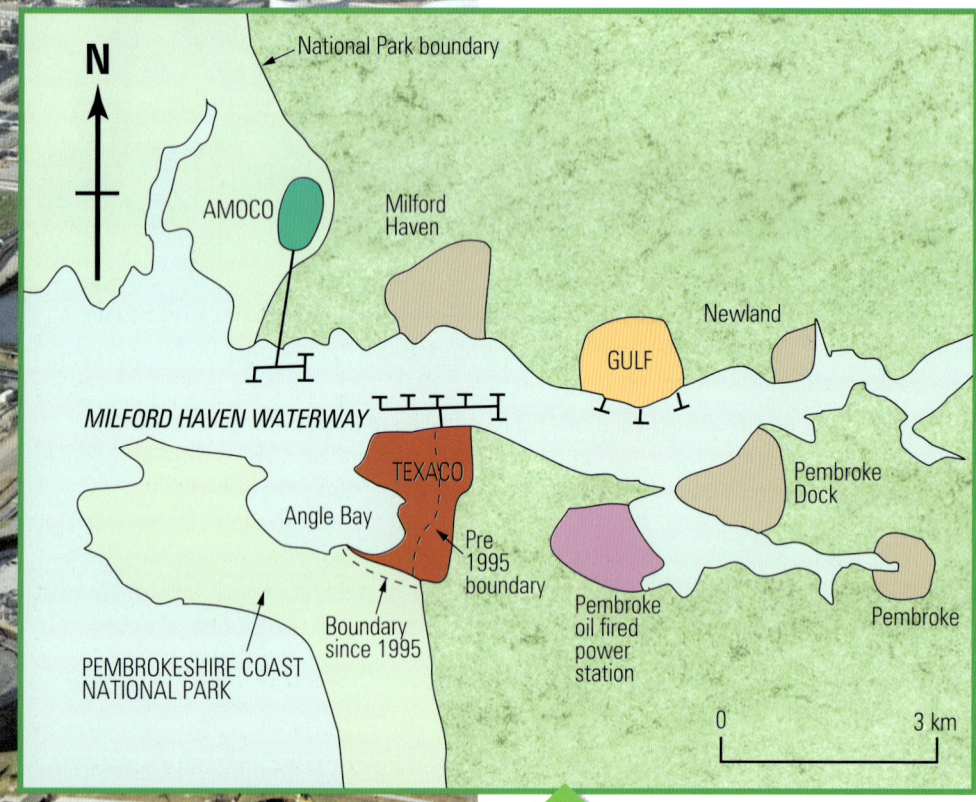

Since the early 1960s a number of oil companies have located along the Milford Haven Waterway (**A**). Most of these refineries lie on the boundary of the Pembrokeshire Coast National Park. Until 1995, 50 per cent of Texaco's refinery lay within the National Park boundary. Then the boundary was altered so that Texaco was no longer in the National Park. All the refineries are important to the local economy and they attempt as far as possible to fit into the local environment.

Why is Milford Haven Waterway a good site for oil refineries?

- The waterway provides a deep water port which can be used by the very large tankers of over 200 000 tonnes.
- The waterway is sheltered from the open sea.
- Milford Haven is close to major worldwide shipping routes as it is located on the western side of the UK.
- The entrance to the waterway is two kilometres wide and there are 112 kilometres of coastline within it. This provides plenty of docking areas and so prevents congestion on this busy stretch of water.
- The waterway is surrounded by flat, cheap land which is suitable for development.
- The area is located away from major centres of population but this has increased distribution costs.

A The location of Texaco within the Milford Haven Waterway

Research Task

1. Write an account of how crude oil is formed. Include the following terms: sedimentary rock, anticline, cap rock, trap and reservoir rock.

2. Where are the world's major sources of crude oil?

4 Economic Activities

National Parks pp6–8
Milford Haven p18
Energy pp70–75

B The oil refining system

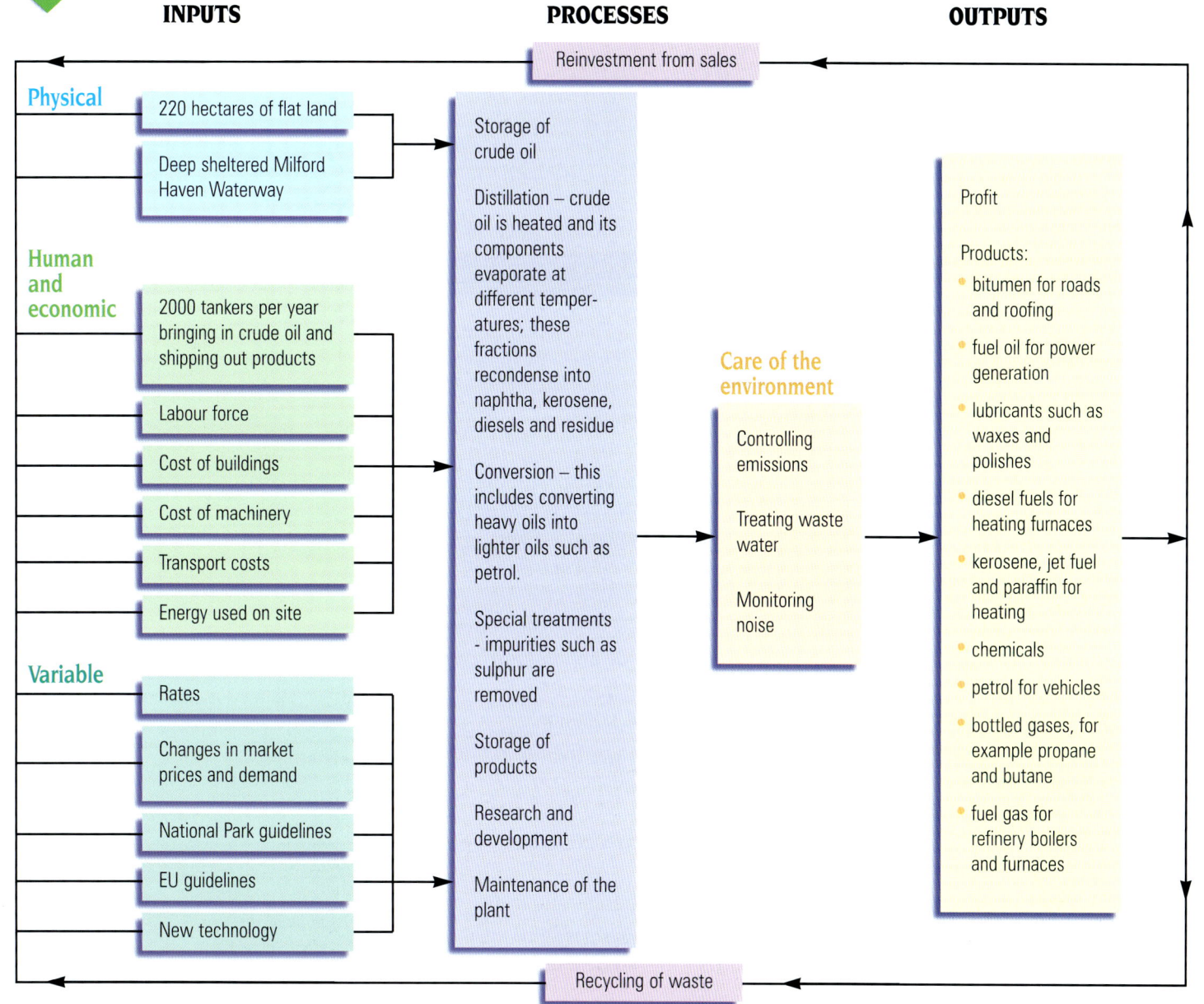

INPUTS

Physical
- 220 hectares of flat land
- Deep sheltered Milford Haven Waterway

Human and economic
- 2000 tankers per year bringing in crude oil and shipping out products
- Labour force
- Cost of buildings
- Cost of machinery
- Transport costs
- Energy used on site

Variable
- Rates
- Changes in market prices and demand
- National Park guidelines
- EU guidelines
- New technology

PROCESSES

- Storage of crude oil
- Distillation – crude oil is heated and its components evaporate at different temperatures; these fractions recondense into naphtha, kerosene, diesels and residue
- Conversion – this includes converting heavy oils into lighter oils such as petrol.
- Special treatments – impurities such as sulphur are removed
- Storage of products
- Research and development
- Maintenance of the plant

Care of the environment
- Controlling emissions
- Treating waste water
- Monitoring noise

OUTPUTS

- Profit
- Products:
  - bitumen for roads and roofing
  - fuel oil for power generation
  - lubricants such as waxes and polishes
  - diesel fuels for heating furnaces
  - kerosene, jet fuel and paraffin for heating
  - chemicals
  - petrol for vehicles
  - bottled gases, for example propane and butane
  - fuel gas for refinery boilers and furnaces

Reinvestment from sales

Recycling of waste

Profile of the oil refinery

Name	Texaco
Opened	1964
Cost	£500 000 000 to build
Size	220 ha (on south bank of waterway)
Operation	24 hours, all year round
Origin of crude oil	North Sea, Persian Gulf, West Africa and Russia
Production	processes 31.5 million litres of crude oil every day, produces 15.4 million litres of petrol every day
Transport of refined products	72% by sea, 26% by pipeline, 2% by road
Employment	550 Texaco employees and approximately 250 long-term contractors
Local environment	Texaco lies just outside the boundary of the National Park; Angle Bay and other local areas adjacent to the refinery have been designated **Sites of Special Scientific Interest** (SSSIs)
Local economy	refinery puts about £29 000 000 into the local economy each year through salaries, rates and local labour

(Source: BTA 1995)

THEMES AND ISSUES: *National Parks in the UK*

Source	%
Industrial discharge and urban runoff	37%
Routine tanker operations	33%
Tanker accidents	12%
Atmosphere	9%
Natural sources	7%
Exploration	2%

C Sources of petroleum in the sea

Environmental care

Since the Texaco refinery was built care for the environment has been an important issue. Many strategies are adopted to minimise the impact of the refinery on the local area. These include:

- Texaco has built raised earth embankments around the refinery to try to minimise the visual impact.
- The colour of the storage tanks is selected to ensure they blend in with the landscape.
- Texaco has a health and safety department which helps to maintain high standards of practice. British Standard BS7750 is followed which states rules for carrying out different activities.
- The air quality is constantly monitored to meet existing laws, although efforts are made to reduce emissions of carbon dioxide, sulphur dioxide and nitrogen oxides below these levels.
- Research into a protozoa is being carried out which will eat pollution.
- The effluent is tested daily in Texaco's own laboratories and by the Environmental Agency. Education and training within the refinery help to ensure correct procedures are obeyed.
- Noise levels are monitored within and around the refinery to check that they are below an agreed limit.
- Waste tips are being reclaimed with extensive planting of grasses and trees.
- A number of contingency plans to deal with major incidents such as oil spills and fires are in place. Drills are carried out regularly to ensure these plans work.

Pollution

The most serious threat of pollution in the Pembrokeshire Coast National Park is from oil, particularly in the Milford Haven Waterway and the Daugleddau estuary. Large-scale spillage is rare, although on a smaller scale accidents do occur. These tend to happen around zones for unloading the crude oil from tankers. Tankers sometimes illegally wash their oil tanks out at sea. These small-scale incidents can lead to oil being washed up onto the shore (**C**). At risk are the sandy beaches and the wildlife habitats (**D**).

The Pembrokeshire County Council have Oil Contingency Emergency Plans to deal with problems. These involve clearing oil from along the open coast and would include help from a number of local and national bodies. A further plan has been set up by the Milford Haven Port Authority to deal with problems in the Milford Haven Waterway. This again requires the co-operation of a number of bodies.

The oil slick was washed ashore covering 190 kilometres of coastline. An oil slick over 20 kilometres long was also seen running north and south of St. Ann's Head.

Effect on the local economy (1) - tourism is a major source of income and in the following summer figures were down by one-third as a result of the disaster.

Effect on the local economy (2) - fishing brings about £20 million a year to the area. On 28 February 1996 the government banned fishing in a 800 square kilometre exclusion zone. Six months later, although it was permitted to catch fish again, the fishing of shell fish remained banned as oil was still present on the sea floor.

4 Economic Activities

BLACK TIDE ENGULFS PEMBROKESHIRE'S MARINE RESERVES

On the evening of 15 February 1996 the *Sea Empress* oil tanker carrying 130 000 tonnes of crude oil was heading for the Texaco oil terminal in the Milford Haven Waterway. At the mouth of the waterway disaster struck - the tanker ran aground off St. Ann's Head.

Over the course of the next six days a number of attempts were made to refloat the tanker. The salvagers were hampered by gale force winds and strong tides. Eventually the *Sea Empress* was pulled clear and taken into dock. The tanker had lost 70 000 tonnes of oil (the tenth largest ever spillage).

(Source: adapted from New Scientist, March 1996)

D Consequences of the oil slick

Loss of wildlife - particularly at risk along this stretch of coastline were the marine nature reserves where there are over a dozen SSSIs and major bird colonies (such as those on Skomer and Skokholm Islands). Thousands of birds, especially guillemots and razorbills, died as a result of oiled feathers.

Financial loss was caused by loss of livelihood and claims to the insurance companies for compensation.

THEMES AND ISSUES: National Parks in the UK

E Diary of the oil slick

1996

15 February	At 8:07 pm the *Sea Empress* ran aground off St. Ann's Head just outside the Milford Haven Waterway. About 1000 tonnes of light crude oil were spilt into the sea. At 10 pm attempts were made to refloat the tanker.
16 February	Four tugs refloated the ship and salvage teams decided how best to remove the remaining oil.
17 February	At 9:30 am the pump room was flooded which delayed the transfer of the remaining oil. The weather was fine but gales were forecast. At 4 pm the tanker was turned around. At 6:30 pm the anchor chains snapped and the tanker ran aground again.
18 February	At 2:30 am weather conditions deteriorated so the tanker was evacuated and the salvage attempts were called off. Extra tugs were ordered to the site.
19 February	At 1 am the tanker position was stabilised but it continued to leak oil. At 7 pm strong tides and gale winds made it impossible for the tugs to hold the tanker which ran aground again. At 11 pm break up of the tanker was expected.
20 February	The tanker continued to leak oil as air was pumped into the tanker to increase its buoyancy.
21 February	At 7 pm the tanker was finally refloated and taken to jetty in Milford Haven. The tanker continued to leak oil.

Three days later on 24 February the remaining oil was pumped off the tanker.

Pembrokeshire's clean sweep

The clean up campaign operated primarily in areas badly affected and those which were important to the tourism industry. The beaches were sprayed and cleaned by hand whilst the sea was sprayed with detergents by aeroplanes. At the same time wildlife was collected and painstakingly cleaned by hand. Texaco has its own cleaning centre and helped the RSPB to return the birds to their natural habitats.

On every high tide more oil was left on the beaches to be cleaned up. Beach patrols constantly monitored the area and issued warnings to the public not to swim when oil levels were too high. Despite the disaster nature has its own way of dealing with problems. The coastline here is a high energy environment, one that receives a lot of powerful sea action which helps to break up the oil. Six months after the spill the coast appeared to be back to normal.

4 Economic Activities

Fa Aerial view of the Texaco refinery

Fb Outline sketch of the refinery

Fc OS map extract of the area

Exam practice

1 Copy the outline sketch of the Texaco refinery and using the aerial view and OS map extract, label the following features:
 - Milford Haven Waterway;
 - jetty;
 - crude oil storage tanks;
 - distillation towers;
 - water storage pool;
 - refined products storage tanks;
 - Pembrokeshire Coast Path;
 - Angle Bay. *(8 marks)*

2 Use the OS map extract and your completed sketch to describe the land use in the area. *(5 marks)*

3 Describe and explain the location of oil refineries. *(6 marks)*

4 'Oil refining brings social and economic gains but can create environmental problems.' Discuss. *(6 marks)*

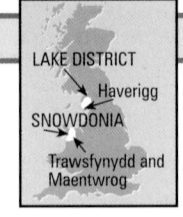

Energy in the National Parks

The demand for electricity in the UK is increasing due to a growth in population and the continued development of technology. Most of the UK's electricity is generated from the burning of **fossil fuels** (**A**). When coal, oil and gas are burnt, carbon dioxide, which is thought to contribute to the greenhouse effect, and sulphur dioxide, which contributes to acid rain, are given off. Fossil fuels are **finite resources** and are being used up much faster than they are being formed. With increasing environmental concern and a limited supply of fossil fuels, alternative sources of energy have to be found. National Parks offer many resources and ideal locations for **renewable energy** schemes.

Trawsfynydd nuclear power station

Trawsfynydd is located by the A470 in the mountainous landscape of Snowdonia National Park (**B**). It is the only nuclear power station in a National Park. Huge amounts of water are used for cooling. Strong foundations are needed to support the heavy reactor.

A quarter of the electricity in England and Wales is produced by nuclear power; in Scotland the proportion is even higher (53 per cent). Nuclear power gives off a negligible amount of carbon dioxide and no sulphur dioxide. However, the radioactive waste gives rise to much controversy. Nuclear power is very efficient and is able to reprocess a large proportion of the fuel, but it is still reliant on a finite resource.

All electricity in the UK

Key
- Fossil fuels (coal, oil and gas) 74%
- Nuclear 24%
- Renewables 2%

Renewable energy in the UK

Key
- Hydroelectric 84%
- Waste (sewage, landfill, and waste combustion) 15%
- Wind 1%

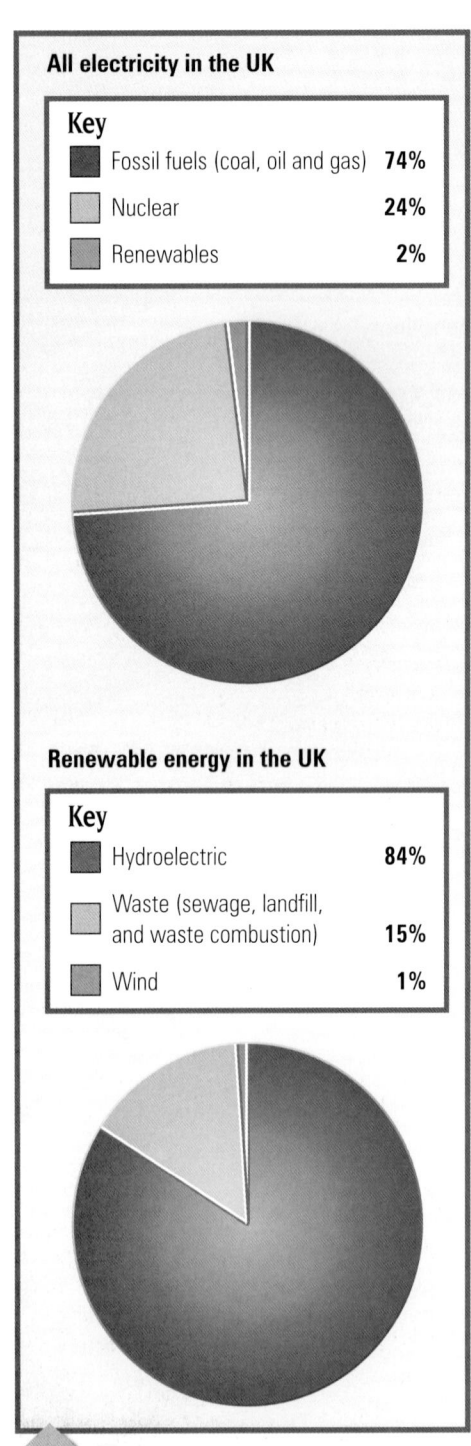

A Sources of electricity in the UK

Nuclear energy facts

- In a nuclear reactor **fission** is controlled and the heat generated is used to produce steam. This turns a turbine to make electricity.
- Nuclear Electric state that 0.5 kilograms of uranium provides the same amount of energy as 1000 tonnes of coal.
- Uranium is highly radioactive only after it has been used. The spent fuel is stored in cooling ponds so that it can cool before it is transported to the Sellafield reprocessing plant.
- Safe generation of nuclear power is the main priority:

– All the safety systems at the plant have several back-up systems which are regularly checked. In the event of problems the automatic shut down facility will close down the reactor in three seconds.

– Samples are taken from the surrounding area and are checked by Nuclear Electric, the Welsh Office, the Department for the Environment and the Ministry of Agriculture, Fisheries and Food. These results are published and show insignificant effects on the background radiation levels.

– Transport of nuclear waste is by 43-tonne flasks which are able to withstand a head-on collision with a train at 160 kph.

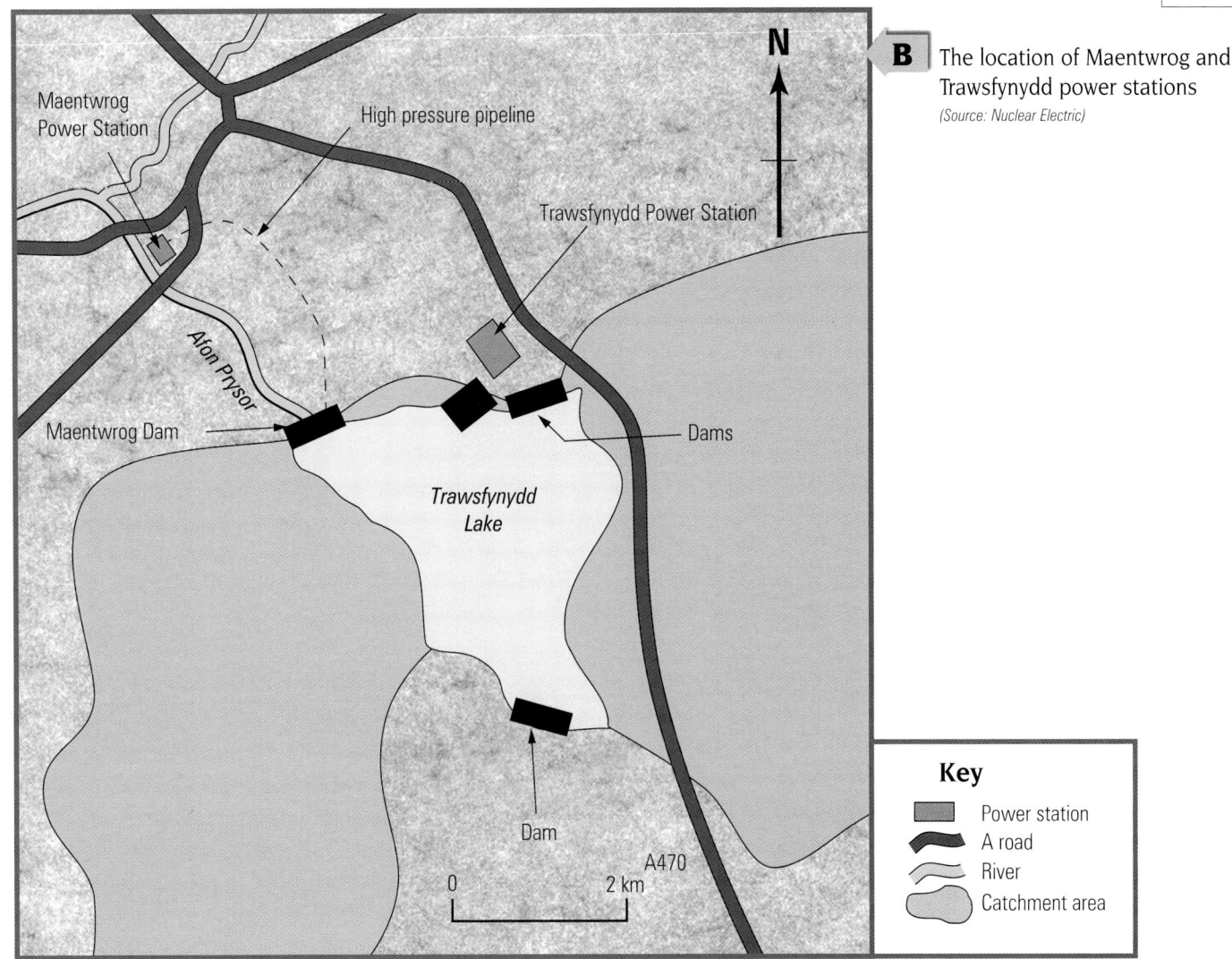

| 4 Economic Activities | National Parks pp6–8
 Glaciation pp10–13
 Texaco pp64–9 |

B The location of Maentwrog and Trawsfynydd power stations
(Source: Nuclear Electric)

Key
- Power station
- A road
- River
- Catchment area

The decommissioning of Trawsfynydd

The nuclear power station at Trawsfynydd opened in 1965 and reached the end of its economic life in 1993. The decommissioning process is now taking place. Eighty plants worldwide have been decommissioned and so it is not a new process. There are several stages in the decommissioning process:

1993–95 All the nuclear fuel was removed from Trawsfynydd. This accounted for 99.9 per cent of the site's radioactivity.

1995–2000 Buildings that are non-radioactive are to be dismantled. The reactor buildings are to be reduced in height and a safe store is to be built; this will completely envelop the main reactor buildings and will be made from durable materials such as concrete, brick and stainless steel.

2001–2127 The safe store will require minimal care and maintenance though routine checks will be carried out.

2128–36 The safe store can be dismantled and the site cleared as the radioactive material will be less hazardous. The area will then be available for other land uses.

During decommissioning the power station continues to offer tours of the site and facilities for the general public and educational visits. The station has set up a creative conservation scheme which helps to increase the wildlife population in the area by encouraging marsh and reed beds at the edge of the lake.

Research Task

Use the information provided and any other additional sources. What are the benefits and costs of nuclear power? Provide a balanced argument and support your answer with factual information.

THEMES AND ISSUES: *National Parks in the UK*

Hydroelectricity at Maentwrog

Maentwrog power station is a small-scale hydroelectric power (HEP) scheme owned by Nuclear Electric (**C**). In the UK about two per cent of all electricity is produced by HEP. However, 84 per cent of all renewable energy comes from HEP (see **A** on page 70), therefore it makes a small but significant contribution to meeting the UK energy demand. Some forms of renewable energy such as HEP and wind power are not new ideas. Once an HEP station has been set up it produces cheap, instant electricity.

The requirements for an HEP station are very specific which means there are only a limited number of suitable sites. These tend to be in upland areas. The location requirements for HEP include:

- an area of reliable rainfall in a large catchment area;
- an area of impermeable bedrock to prevent water seepage underground;
- a suitable site for constructing a reservoir - reasonably steep valley sides with a narrow section for the dam to be built (the reservoir is dammed to store and regulate water flow to the HEP station);
- a steep gradient between the reservoir and the HEP station which has the potential to produce large amounts of energy.

The history of Maentwrog

In 1924 the Maentwrog Dam was built across the Afon Prysor to create Lake Trawsfynydd. Three further dams were built to contain the water in the lake. The lake covers 506 hectares and contains 33 million cubic metres of water which is used to produce HEP at Maentwrog. The catchment area of the lake has up to 2790 millimetres of rainfall per year covering an area of about 90 square kilometres. In 1989 the old Maentwrog Dam was rebuilt to extend the economic life of the HEP station a further 60 years.

Making hydroelectric power

- The Maentwrog Dam is located 185 metres above the HEP station (**D**).
- Water from the lake travels over 1.6 kilometres to the station by pipeline.
- The two turbines in the HEP station can each receive 21 000 litres of water per second.
- This water rotates the turbines which turn the rotor in the generator to produce electricity.
- The station produces 30 megawatts of electricity which is fed into the **National Grid**.

C Maentwrog HEP station and the high pressure pipelines

Protecting the environment

The Maentwrog Dam is located close to the Ceunant Llennyrch Gorge, a **Site of Special Scientific Interest**. Within this area there is also a National Nature Reserve to protect many rare species of plant. One of Nuclear Electric's main priorities is to preserve the landscape and ensure the lake continues to be a suitable habitat for wildlife.

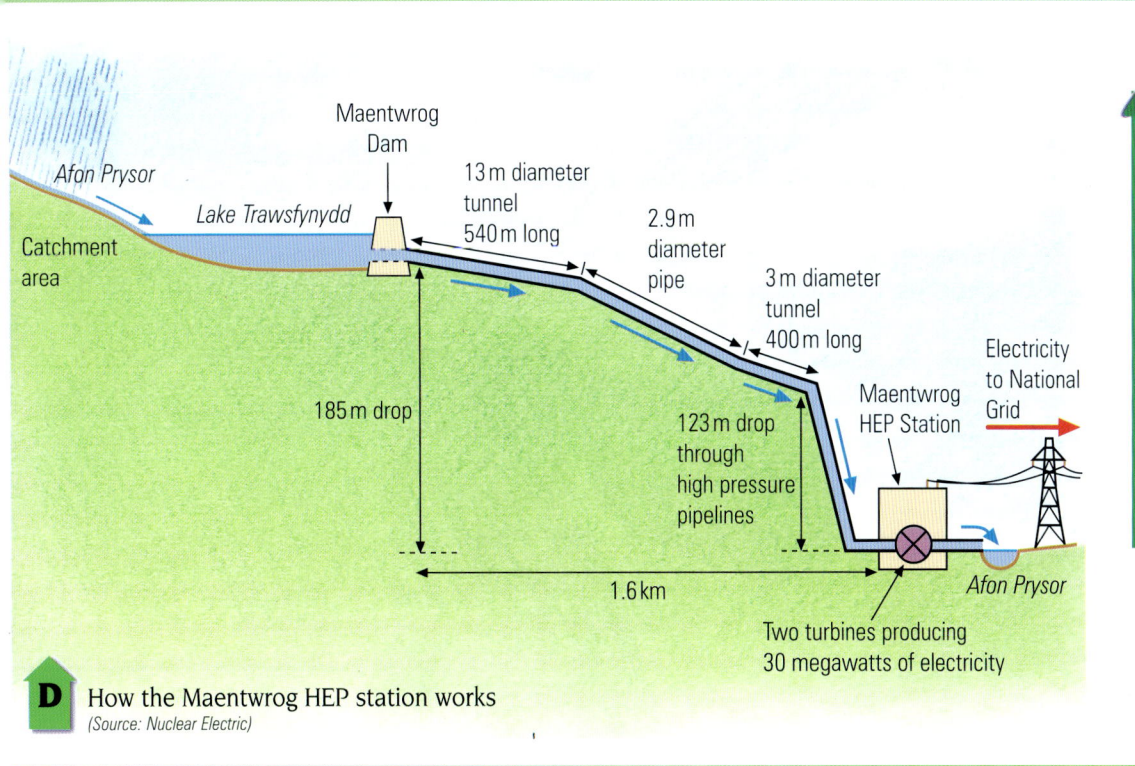

4 Economic Activities

D How the Maentwrog HEP station works
(Source: Nuclear Electric)

Activities

1. Renewable sources of energy are increasingly being used to produce electricity. With reference to specific examples explain why the UK is developing alternative sources of energy.

2. Describe the advantages of Maentwrog as a location for an HEP station.

Wind power

The physical characteristics of many of the National Parks with their upland areas and high wind speeds provide suitable environments for the development of wind power. However, there are many concerns over the environmental impact of building wind turbines in the National Parks.

Wind speeds of over five metres per second are needed to locate a wind turbine and for it to be cost effective. Turbines are able to convert 45 per cent of the wind power into electricity. The government has estimated that 20 000 wind turbines covering 30 000 square kilometres would be needed to produce 10 per cent of the UK's energy.

Wind energy in the National Parks

National Park Authorities do not permit the development of large-scale wind farms. (Two or more turbines are classed as a large-scale development.)

Single turbines can be found throughout many of the parks which meet the needs of an individual farmer or hamlet. Even these small-scale developments are subject to strict constraints to protect the landscape. Each application for a wind turbine is carefully considered to ensure that the negative effects do not outweigh the benefits.

Haverigg in Cumbria

Haverigg is a wind farm located one kilometre outside the Lake District National Park boundary (**E**). The turbines were built on a disused airfield 200 metres from the sea and ten metres above sea level. It is jointly owned by Windcluster Limited and PowerGen plc. The site consists of five turbines but the owners have permission to build four more on the same site. The electricity produced is fed into the National Grid.

E Haverigg wind farm with the Lake District National Park in the background

THEMES AND ISSUES: **National Parks in the UK**

Decision making exercise – Locating a wind farm

It has been decided to build a wind farm with five turbines in the area shown in the two maps (**F**). Three sites have been suggested; all have advantages and disadvantages. Study the maps carefully and use any other information in this chapter to answer the questions opposite.

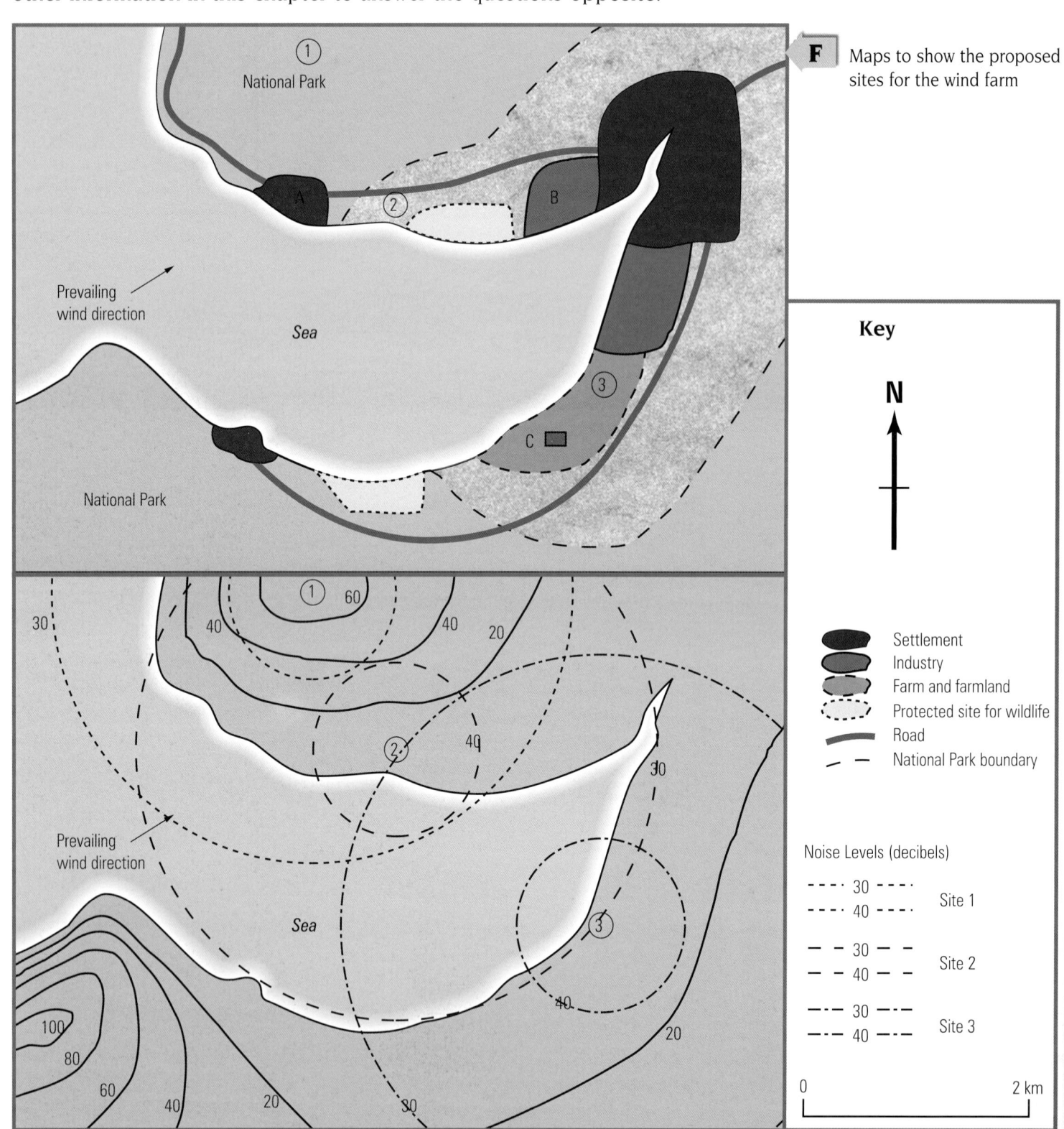

F Maps to show the proposed sites for the wind farm

Key

- Settlement
- Industry
- Farm and farmland
- Protected site for wildlife
- Road
- National Park boundary

Noise Levels (decibels)
- ---- 30 ---- / ---- 40 ---- Site 1
- – 30 – / – 40 – Site 2
- –·– 30 –·– / –··– 40 –··– Site 3

0 — 2 km

74

4 Economic Activities

Pros
It is a renewable form of energy which does not give off harmful gases.

The turbines will last for up to 20 years and are easy to dismantle if the land is to be returned to its former use.

A survey of the people living near wind farms found that 75 per cent had a positive attitude to further developments.

Small groups of carefully located wind turbines would have a reduced environmental impact.

Wind farms provide employment and have become tourist attractions offering opportunities for education.

Cons
Wind turbines produce relatively expensive electricity, although the price may decrease as the industry grows.

They can have a strong visual impact on the landscape.

Inspectors from the Department of the Environment suggest that between 30 and 40 decibels is the noise limit for wind farms. In a letter to the *Daily Telegraph* on 21 October 1993 it was reported that noise levels any higher would have a human cost.

G The pros and cons of wind energy

1. Why is it important for the UK to find renewable sources of energy? *(2 marks)*

2. Why are most sources of energy turned into electricity before being used? *(2 marks)*

3. What are the advantages and disadvantages of using wind power to make electricity? *(4 marks)*

4. What factors would the developers of the new wind farm have to consider when selecting a site? *(5 marks)*

5. What would the views of the following people be on each of the three sites:
   - resident of village A;
   - local industry manager working at B;
   - local farmer at C;
   - representative of the National Park Authority? *(6 marks)*

6. Which of the three sites would you choose for the wind farm? Explain your choice. *(6 marks)*

Tourism – a tertiary industry

One of the aims of the National Parks is to promote the enjoyment of these areas. Tourism has therefore played an important role in the development of National Parks. Tourism provides services for people, so is an example of a tertiary industry.

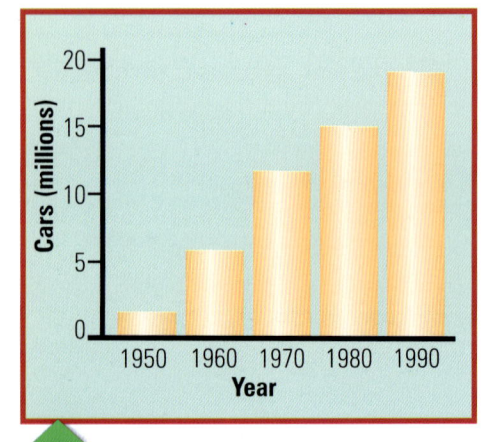

A The increase in the number of cars in the UK

Since the National Parks were set up the number of activities they offer has gradually increased. The parks were originally used by people, escaping from urban areas, who wanted to enjoy the peace and quiet of the countryside. They tended to take part in traditional activities such as walking, camping and climbing. With increased car ownership (**A**) less active people began to visit the parks to enjoy the scenery, browse around **honeypot** sites and go for short strolls. This encouraged road development and the provision of more services. Activities within the parks have become more varied and now include hang-gliding, windsurfing and water-skiing. The leisure industry has continued to grow with an increased demand for hotels, health spas, golf courses and other private enterprises.

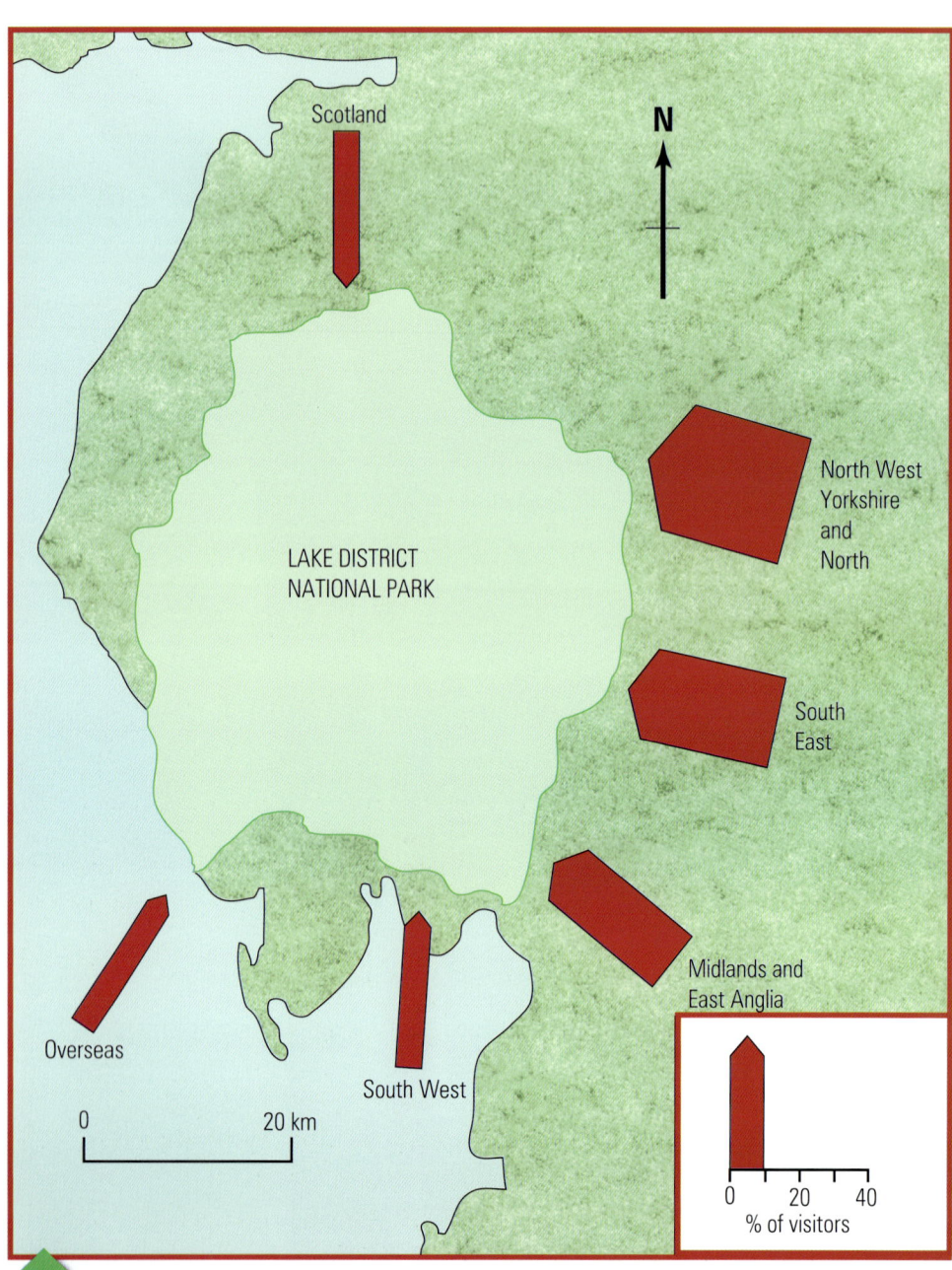

B The origin of visitors to the Lake District National Park
(Source: Lake District National Park Authority)

4 **Economic Activities**

National Parks	pp6–8
Snowdonia	pp10–13
Yorkshire Dales	p23
Upper Derwent valley	p27
The Broads	p29
Castleton	pp38–43
Accessibility	pp44–5
Okehampton	p46
Camping barns	p56
Dunster	p89
Exmoor	p91
Planning and development	pp92–3

Reasons for the increase in tourism:
- There has been an increase in car ownership.
- Road networks have improved making the National Parks more accessible.
- More people are taking short breaks due to the stress of modern living.
- Increased wealth means that more people can afford to go away.
- The population has increased so there is a greater demand for leisure.

The Lake District National Park

Surveys show the Lake District to be the most popular summer destination for short breaks. It receives approximately 12 million visitors a year – 9 million come for a day out and the other 3 million stay at least one night. Ninety per cent of visitors arrive by car. The impact of tourism is a major issue affecting the Lake District. The Lake District's popularity is due to the beautiful scenery, lakes, mountains and wild landscape as well as many attractive towns and villages.

Tourism and the economy

Almost half the population of the Lake District is employed in the tourist industry. Tourism is a vital source of employment and income in the area. Over 20 000 jobs are as a direct result of tourism; half of these are seasonal or part-time. Over two-thirds of this employment is found in the areas around Windermere and Keswick. Tourists spend approximately £350 million per year.

Whilst tourism is an essential part of the Lake District economy, conflicts and problems can arise. It is therefore important to achieve a balance between promoting people's enjoyment of the countryside and preserving the landscape.

Tourism initiatives in the Lake District National Park

The National Park Authority has encouraged a number of strategies to control the land use and tourism within the park (see **F** on page 79).

- Three main quiet areas within the park have been established. This will retain the traditional character of these areas. Facilities which encourage large numbers of visitors are not allowed. A **negative planning technique** is employed; roads to Wastwater, for example, will not be improved or upgraded. The limited car parking and narrow, windy lanes will encourage people to walk.
- There are two main corridors of access into the Lake District in which tourism is focused; these are along the A66 (Penrith to Keswick) and the A591 (Kendal to Keswick). These roads have been upgraded and parking facilities have been provided. Caravan sites are concentrated within this area so they are easily accessible and do not result in congestion on the narrow roads.
- The high levels of activity in the busier **honeypot** areas of the National Park will be contained and are not allowed to spread to the quieter areas.
- The National Park Authority will look favourably at development proposals that encourage people's appreciation of the Lake District.

Agriculture, forestry and fishing	**9.9%**
Energy, water supply and mining	**4.7%**
Industry, manufacturing and construction	**16.8%**
Retailing, hotels and catering	**34.5%**
Transport and communications	**3%**
Other services	**31.1%**

C Employment figures for the Lake District, 1991
(Source: Corporate Information Unit, CCC)

Activities

1. Select a suitable graph to display the data in **C**.

2. Where do the majority of visitors to the Lake District come from (see **B**)?

3. Why has the number of people visiting National Parks increased?

77

Themes and Issues: *National Parks in the UK*

D A developed area within the Lake District

E A quiet area within the Lake District

- The lakes have been classified into the developed lakes, which will be managed, and natural lakes. The natural lakes are only allowed to be used by the lakeside owners and may include conservation sites and **Sites of Special Scientific Interest**. The managed lakes include the larger ones where certain activities are permitted. For example, boating is allowed on a large scale at the more accessible lakes such as Coniston Water, Derwent Water, Ullswater and Windermere. Windermere is the only lake that allows the use of private motor boats. The speed limit is 16 kilometres per hour across the lake with the exception of the water-skiing zone. To minimise noise silencers must be used on boats.

- The Lake District Traffic Management Initiative was submitted in 1995 and outlined a number of proposals. The roads were to be classified, restricting their use to specific vehicle groups, **park and ride schemes** were to be set up and use of public transport was to be encouraged.

- The National Park Authority recognises the importance of tourism and the need to develop strategies to maintain the number of visitors.

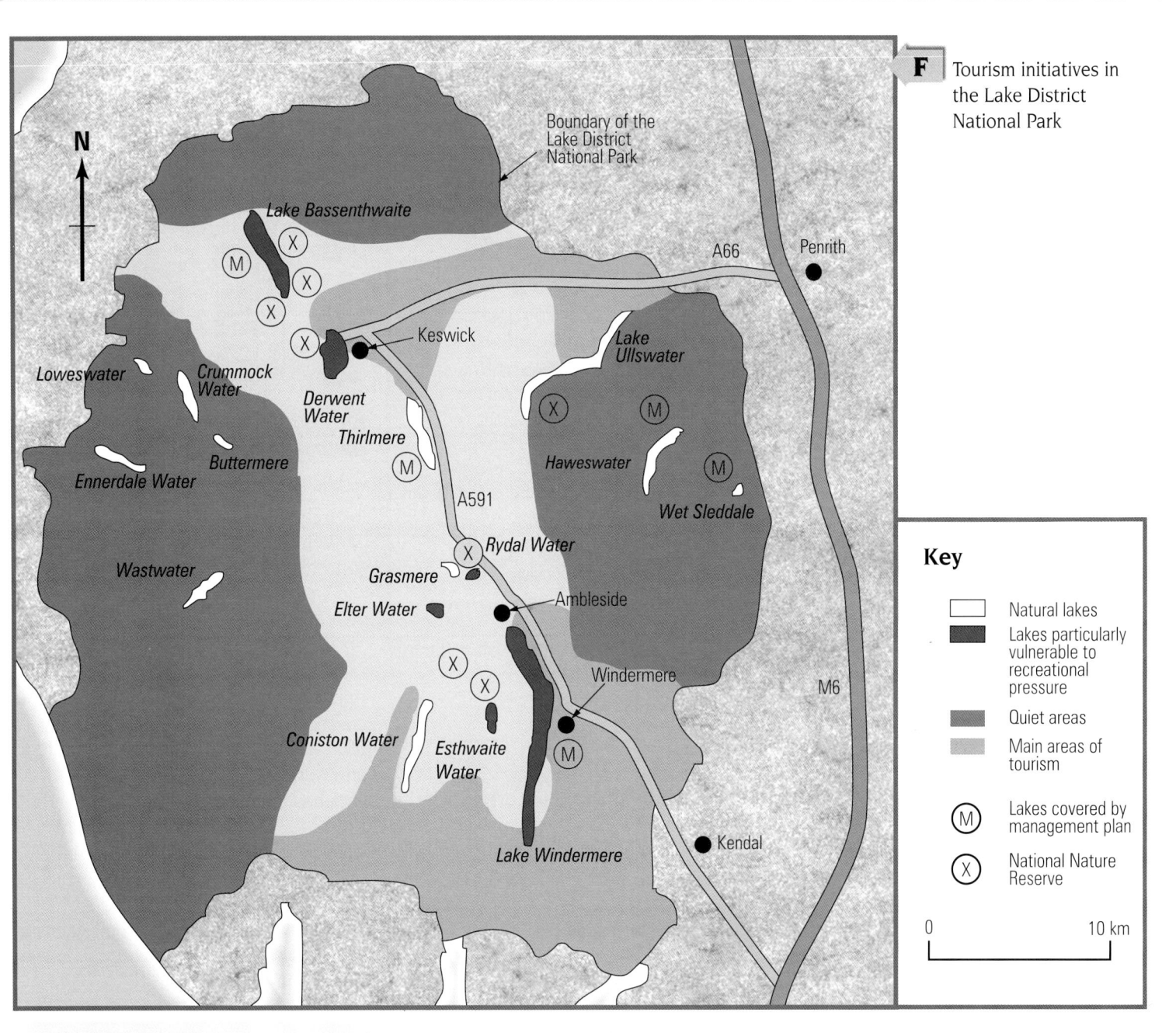

4 Economic Activities

F Tourism initiatives in the Lake District National Park

Key
- Natural lakes
- Lakes particularly vulnerable to recreational pressure
- Quiet areas
- Main areas of tourism
- Ⓜ Lakes covered by management plan
- Ⓧ National Nature Reserve

0 — 10 km

Exam practice

1. Describe how the physical features of the Lake District have encouraged tourism and leisure activities. *(4 marks)*

2. Explain how an increase in the number of tourists affects the physical environment of the Lake District. Mention both positive and negative points. *(4 marks)*

3. Tourism has brought advantages and disadvantages for the economy. Explain this statement using the Lake District to illustrate your answer. *(4 marks)*

4. The increasing use of the Lake District has brought about many conflicts. Describe in detail two examples and the solutions planners can adopt to deal with these problems. *(4 marks)*

5. Using photographs **D** and **E** describe the opportunity for recreational activity and the management strategies used. *(4 marks)*

Themes and Issues: National Parks in the UK

G Facilities for tourists around Lake Windermere

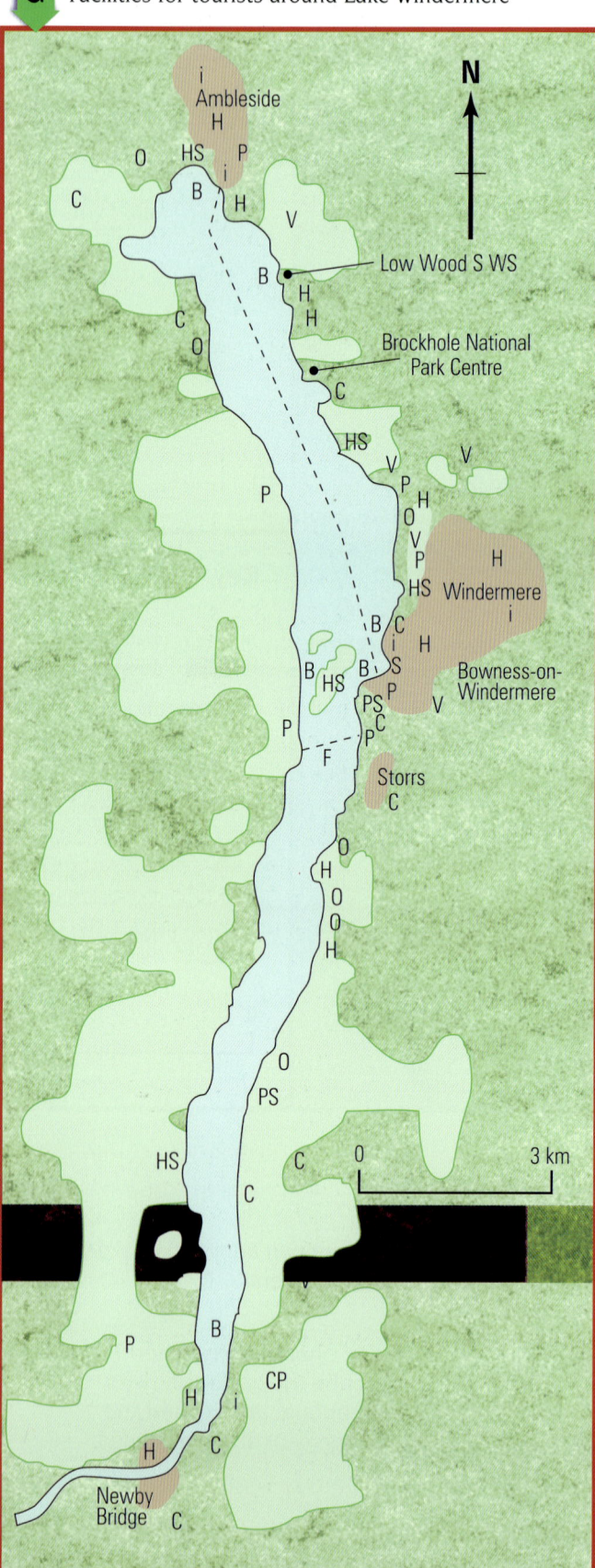

Key

	Lake Windermere
	Settlement
i	Information centre
O	Outdoor pursuits centre
P	Parking
B	Boating facilities
WS	Water Skiing
S	Sailing club
v	View point
C	Caravan and / or camping site
	Forest / woodland
HS	Historic Site / Museum
F	Ferry
PS	Picnic Site
CP	Country Park
H	Hotel

Windermere – a honeypot

Windermere, England's largest lake, is located in the southern Lake District. Windermere and Bowness have merged to form the largest tourist attraction in the Lake District National Park. Each year 3 million tourists visit this area. These tourists are provided with a wide range of services (**G**) within an area of outstanding beauty. It is a commercial centre that relies on the money the tourists spend on accommodation, food and drink, boat trips and local goods. This has increased the prosperity of the two towns. As with many **honeypot** sites problems and conflicts occur. The majority of visitors arrive by car which leads to traffic congestion and a shortage of parking spaces (**H**). Another major issue within this area is the buying of **second homes**.

H Congestion in Bowness-on-Windermere

4 Economic Activities

I The impact of second homes
(Source: Simmonds, 1985)

Second homes

The number of second homes and holiday homes has gradually increased in Windermere and Bowness. Holiday homes are those that are rented out on a commercial basis to many different people. Second homes are usually owned by a family that lives elsewhere. They are used mainly by that family and their friends. The percentage of holiday homes and second homes varies greatly around the different areas of the Lake District. The highest concentration is found along the two tourist corridors (see **F** on page 79). Windermere has a total of 4582 dwellings, of which 372 are second homes and 355 are holiday homes. In summary, 14 per cent of dwellings are not permanently lived in. The use of these types of homes brings many benefits to the area but does have its costs.

Benefits
- Buying a second home injects money into the area and provides employment for solicitors and estate agents.
- Many second home owners make improvements to their property. This can provide employment to the local building industry and the renovation of run-down houses can improve the landscape.
- The owners will spend money in the local area and so contribute to the economy.
- Rates will be paid on the property but there will be little use of the services provided.
- Second homes may revive a village where many of the locals have moved elsewhere.
- The users of the property are able to escape from urban life to a relaxed atmosphere.

Costs
- The buying of second homes leads to more competition and this in turn increases local house prices. Many locals cannot afford these inflated amounts.
- Money spent in the area creates low-paid seasonal jobs.
- If the homes were occupied by permanent residents their expenditure in the local area would be much higher.
- The local services are not used due to a decreased demand. Schools could close and public transport be withdrawn. However, more services would be needed during peak season.
- The community spirit and the rural way of life is threatened by the influx of strangers.
- Locals may envy the wealth of the visitors.
- Improvements may not always be in keeping with other local buildings leading to a change in the character of the area.

Exam practice

1 Explain the meaning of the phrase 'a tourist honeypot'. (2 marks)

2 Why has Windermere become a tourist honeypot? (6 marks)

3a Suggest reasons for the traffic congestion by Lake Windermere as shown in **H**. (4 marks)

b How could this congestion be reduced? (2 marks)

4 How will the increasing number of second homes affect Windermere? (6 marks)

5 Using the cartoon in **I**, describe the effects of people buying second homes. (4 marks)

THEMES AND ISSUES: **National Parks in the UK**

The pressure of tourism – Footpath erosion

Footpath erosion is one of the most topical issues affecting all the National Park landscapes. With the huge increase in tourism and in the popularity of hill walking, rock climbing and rambling, there has been a growth and deterioration of upland footpaths.

The Brecon Beacons

The Brecon Beacon range of mountains is composed of old red sandstone. The sandstone was formed about 400 million years ago by the deposition of sediment in rivers and deltas. This sedimentary rock was then folded and raised by earth movements. A plateau was formed which was eroded by glaciers during the Ice Age to leave steep north facing slopes and a number of corries, such as Cwm-Llwch. The highest point of the Beacons is the mountain of Pen-y-fan (886 metres).

Rainfall is 2300 millimetres per year on average, although more rainfall is received in higher upland areas. The soils are generally thin, particularly on the steeper summit slopes. These soils tend to be sandy. If the sandy soils are exposed they are eroded more easily, especially with the high levels of rainfall.

There has been human activity in the hills of the Brecon Beacons for thousands of years. In the early times the slopes were cleared of woodland and used for grazing. The Romans built routes across the area whilst stone was quarried in more recent centuries.

In the last 40 years the Beacons have become increasingly popular, largely because they are close to the populations of South Wales and the Midlands. Surveys carried out by the Brecon Beacon National Park estimated that about 60 000 people walked the highest mountains, Pen-y-fan and Corn Du, each year (**J**). The area is also used by the army for training purposes. This recreational pressure has led to the development of new paths and the erosion of the most well used ones.

Ja Footpath erosion on the slopes of Pen-y-fan and Corn Du

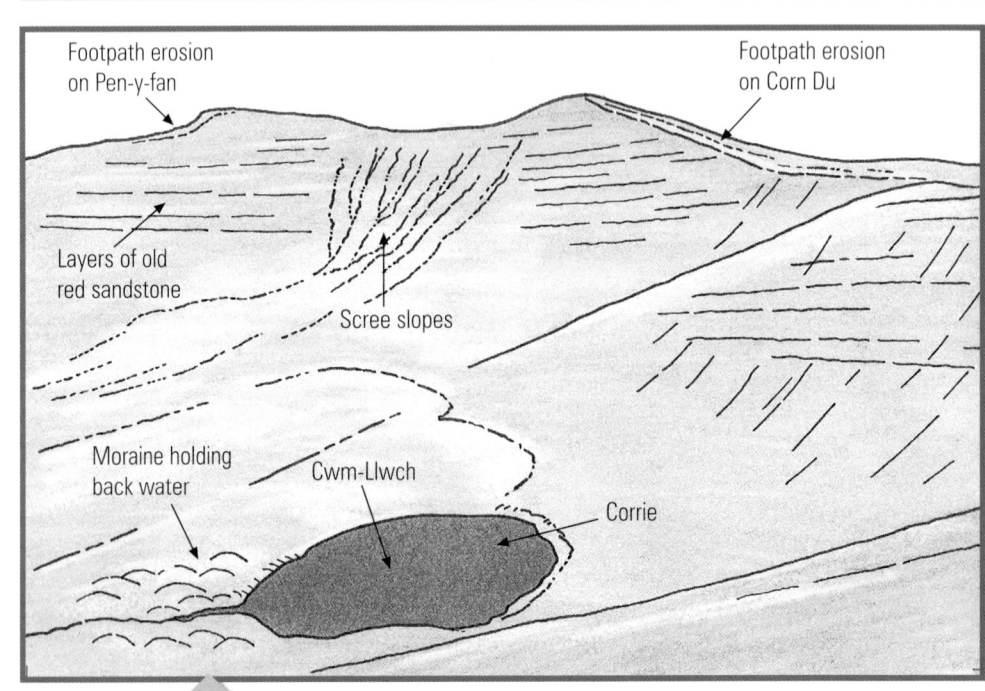

Jb Sketch to highlight the main features from **Ja**

82

4 Economic Activities

The process of footpath erosion:
- The vegetation is trampled and the soil compacted along the footpath.
- The vegetation dies leaving bare soil. The harsh climate and poor soils do not allow the vegetation to recover each year.
- The bare soil is washed away by heavy rain which leads to the development of gullies (deeply cut channels).
- The original path becomes difficult to walk on so trampling begins at the side of the original path and the process starts again.

The Brecon Beacons' solution to footpath erosion

The National Trust owns about 4000 hectares of the central area of the Brecon Beacons and has begun a programme of footpath restoration to combat increasing erosion on the summit slopes. The National Trust is assisted by a large number of volunteers. The aim of restoration is to reduce both vegetation loss and the visual impact on the landscape. The repair work is done in two stages (**L**).

FACTORS WHICH CAUSE EROSION

Recreational pressure — The intensity of footpath use will vary according to the attractiveness of the area and the seasonal, weekly and daily fluctuations.

Slope angle — The greater the angle the more erosion will occur (particularly angles greater than 18°).

Surface water — Heavy rain or channelling of water can have strong erosive power.

Frost heave — When water freezes within the soil, the soil particles expand pushing upwards. When the soil thaws it is loosened and is easily eroded.

Vegetation type — Some vegetation types are able to withstand trampling better than others.

Exposure to wind — Soils which are loosened can be blown or washed away more easily.

Soil type — Certain soils are more prone to erosion (e.g. peat) and soil characteristics can affect the rate of erosion (e.g. particle size, stoniness).

K

Stage 1
- Drainage – attempts are made to control and disperse the effects of water. This is done by using culverts (drainage channels) to remove water from the path and ditches to catch the water from the culverts.
- Path construction – pitching is the technique that uses stone placed into the ground to create a hard surface. Where possible the surface is sloped so water can drain away.

Stage 1: plan view — Vegetation, Path, Water, Culverts, Water drains, Main drainage channel

Stage 2
- Landscaping and regenerating – the scar left by erosion is levelled by cutting the surrounding banks down. Netting is used to stop fine soil being washed away and this also protects the growing vegetation. The soil is seeded and stones are left on areas either side of the new path to stop people from straying.

Stage 2: profile — Netting to protect the soil and vegetation, Path, Slope to help drainage, Drainage channel

L Controlling footpath erosion

Between 1990 and 1994 the National Trust was able to repair over seven kilometres of footpath. Work continues and monitoring of the area keeps a check on the paths. The National Trust relies on funds from the Countryside Council for Wales which enables the work to be carried out.

Activities
1. How does footpath erosion occur?
2. What factors lead to footpath erosion (see **K**)?
3. What visual impact do footpaths have on the environment?
4. How can footpath erosion be reduced?

83

THEMES AND ISSUES: National Parks in the UK

Fieldwork task: assessing footpath erosion

Choose an area which is visited by a large number of people each year. This does not have to be in a National Park, but could be a local country park. This task investigates what factors affect footpath erosion in your chosen area (see **K** on page 83).

Method

The equipment needed to carry out this fieldwork task includes: a tape measure, a quadrat, two ranging poles and a clinometer.

1. Measure five sites along a path which will be ten metres apart as follows (see **M**):
   - Measure the width of the path at each site.
   - Place a quadrat at the centre of the path and estimate the percentage vegetation cover and percentage bare earth.
   - Take four more quadrat readings to one side only at one metre intervals, each time moving further away from the centre of the path.
   - Then measure ten metres along the path and repeat the same tasks. Continue to do this until you have surveyed five sites.

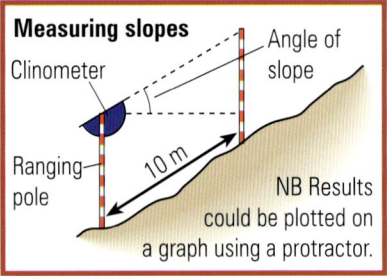

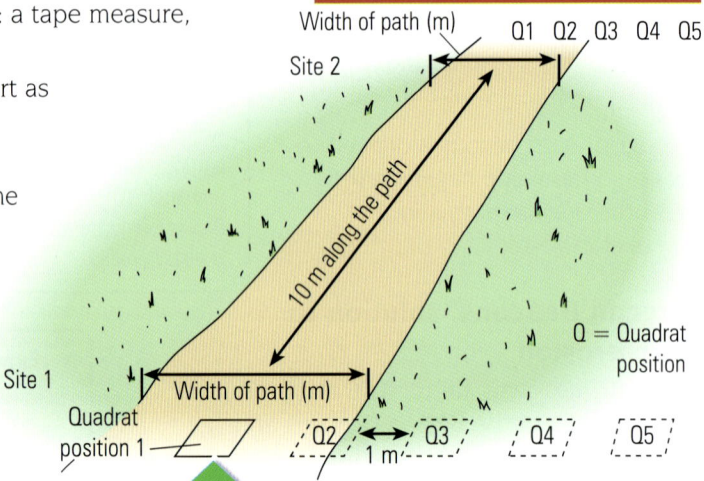

Measuring slopes — Clinometer, Ranging pole, Angle of slope, 10 m. NB Results could be plotted on a graph using a protractor.

M Footpath erosion fieldwork technique

2. Record your results in a table. An example has been given for you in **N**.

DISTANCE ALONG THE PATH		DISTANCE FROM THE MIDDLE OF THE PATH					Width of path	Other observations
		0 m	1 m	2 m	3 m	4 m		
0 m	% veg.							
	% bare earth							
10 m	% veg.							
	% bare earth							
20 m	% veg.							
	% bare earth							
30 m	% veg.							
	% bare earth							
40 m	% veg.							
	% bare earth							

N Results table

3. At any point along the footpath carry out the following tasks:
   - Count how many people use the path in a 15 minute period.
   - Measure the slope angle of the path using the ranging poles, clinometer and tape measure.
4. Draw graphs to show your results.
5. Describe and explain your results.

Extension activity

The steeper the slope the more erosion will take place. You could therefore survey a number of sites of different gradients to test this hypothesis.

5 EXMOOR NATIONAL PARK

Exmoor was designated a National Park in 1954. Whilst it is one of the smallest parks, it has a wide variety of semi-natural habitats. Exmoor includes moorland, wooded valleys known as **combes** (A), and a Heritage Coastline of outstanding beauty. The coast has England's highest cliffs, huge caves, inlets and pebbly beaches (C). Exmoor ponies and wild red deer roam the area. The centre of Exmoor is remote and not easily accessible. The park covers 692 square kilometres of which 29 per cent is in Devon and 71 per cent in Somerset.

People have occupied this area for thousands of years and have therefore helped shape the landscape. Today 10 624 people live and work in the area. Half this population live in the small towns of Dulverton, Dunster, Porlock and Lynton whilst others live in small villages, hamlets and farmsteads. The main source of income used to be sheep farming but is now tourism.

A A combe (the field would once have been wooded)

The National Park Officer manages the park with the help of a deputy and 75 full- and part-time specialist staff. Responsibility is divided into four main areas:

Park management	Planning	Visitor services	Support services
National Park Plan	Development control	Visitor centres	Estimates and budgeting
Ecological surveys	Local plans	Ranger services	Clerical work
Archaeology	Conservation areas and listed buildings	Interpretation and education	Design and cartography
Farming liaison	Village improvement grants	Publications	Caretaking and store keeping
Footpaths and car parks	Enforcement of planning regulations	Rights of way	Information technology
Woodland management			

B The jobs of the Exmoor National Park Authority
(Source: Exmoor National Park Authority, 1993)

C Porlock Bay

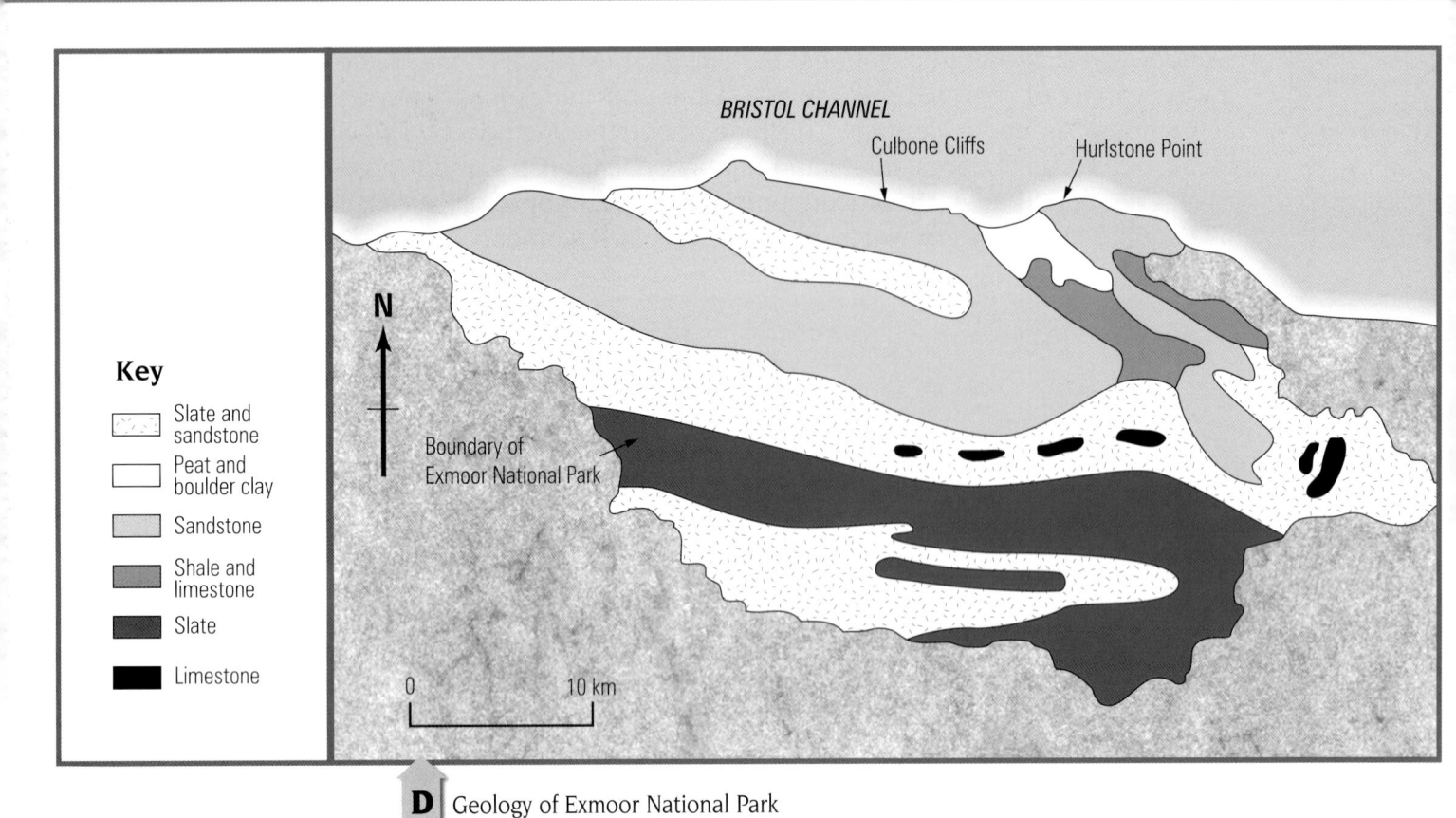

THEMES AND ISSUES: *National Parks in the UK*

Key
- Slate and sandstone
- Peat and boulder clay
- Sandstone
- Shale and limestone
- Slate
- Limestone

D Geology of Exmoor National Park

Key Height in metres
- 0 – 150
- 150 – 300
- 300 – 450
- River
- 1000 Annual rainfall (mm)

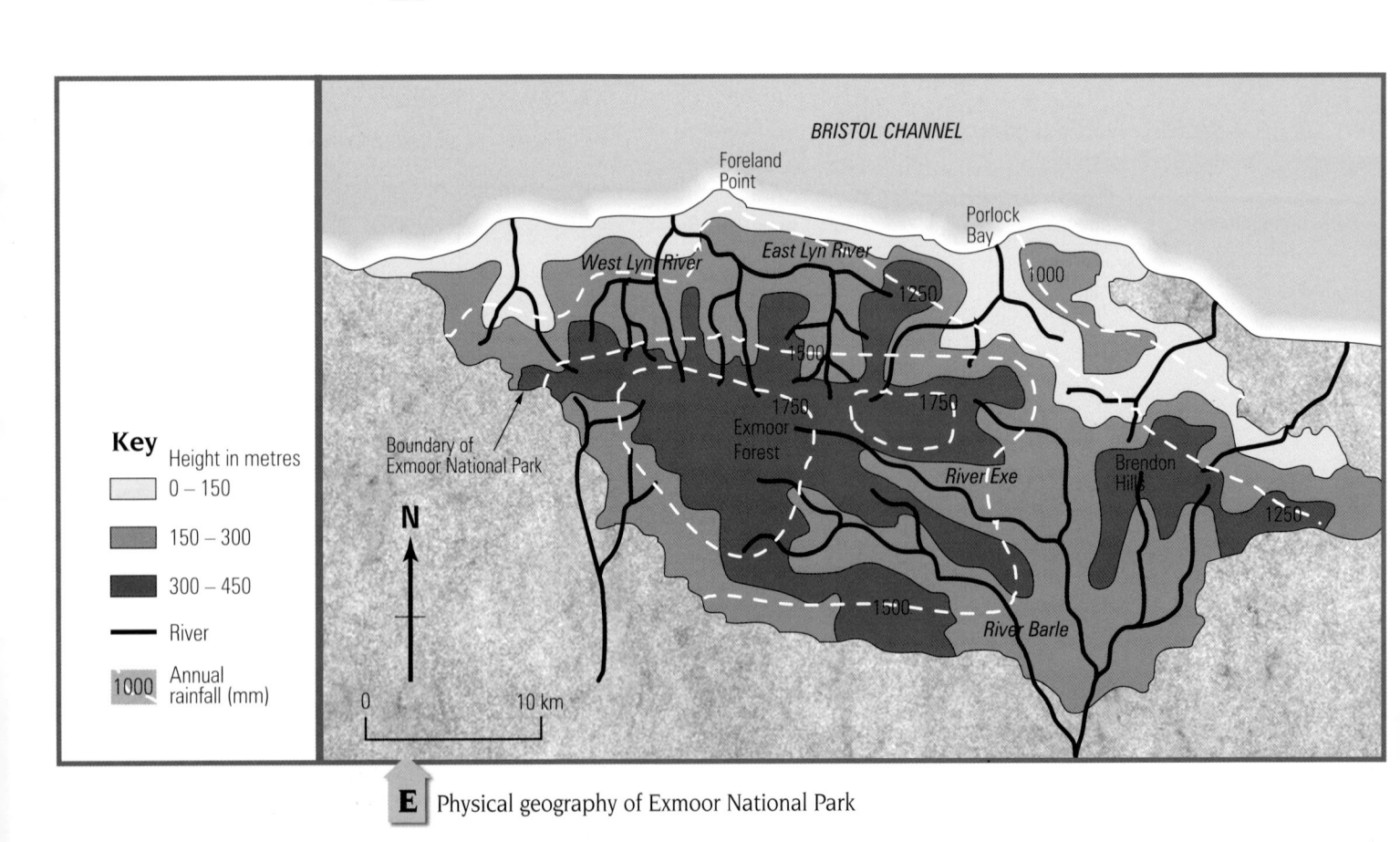

E Physical geography of Exmoor National Park

5 Exmoor National Park

National Parks	pp6–8
Flooding	p28
Castleton	pp38–42
Farming	pp52–5
Tourism	pp76–84

Exmoor National Park consists mainly of sedimentary rock. About 300 million years ago mud and sand on the sea bed was compressed and forced to rise by earth movements. The layers of rock were tilted to form bands of sandstone, limestone, shale and slate (**D**).

The geology influences the characteristic landforms and uses of the area. The rock at Hurlstone Point and Culbone cliffs is harder and more resistant than that found in Porlock Bay (**B** and **D**). In the past quarries and mines were used to obtain local stone, lime and ore. Mining no longer takes place in Exmoor. The red sandstone which makes up most of Exmoor gives well drained soils. In other areas the rocks give rise to wet, **peaty** soils where little will grow.

F Exebridge near Dulverton, Exmoor

G Land use of Exmoor National Park

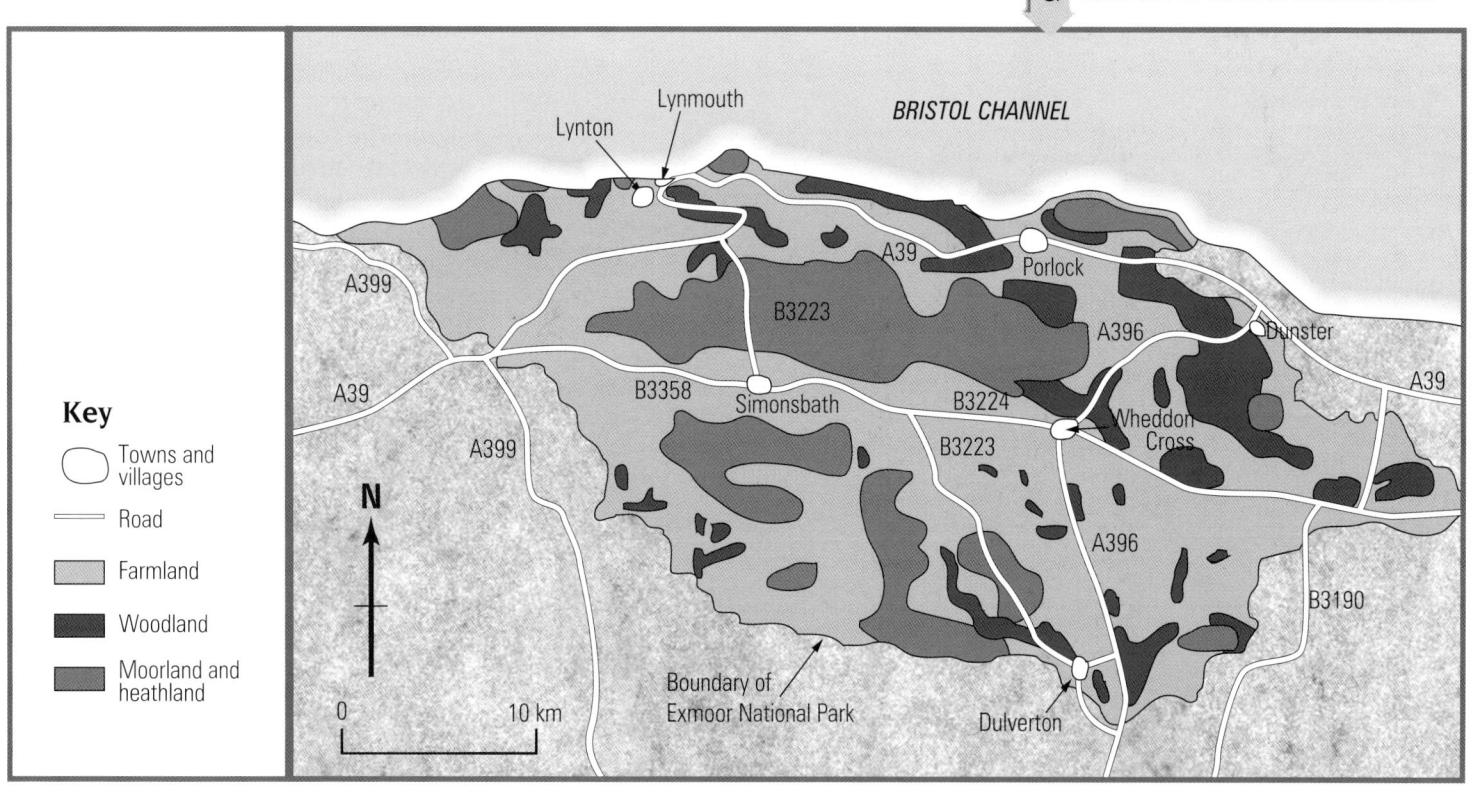

Key
- Towns and villages
- Road
- Farmland
- Woodland
- Moorland and heathland

87

THEMES AND ISSUES: **National Parks in the UK**

Water erosion and flooding in Exmoor

Water erosion

The high rainfall in Exmoor, over 2000 millimetres a year, means that the area is prone to water erosion:

- Footpath erosion due to visitor pressure is accelerated by large amounts of surface water. Temporary streams form in the paths and wash the top soil away.
- After the moorland is burnt the exposed **peat** is easily washed away by the rainfall.
- Many fields are drained which allows water to run off more quickly. This increases the flow of nearby streams. Erosion of the river banks becomes more rapid.

The Lynmouth floods of 1952

On 15 August 1952, 230 millimetres of rain fell in the catchment of the East and West Lyn Rivers (see **E** on page 86). The wet summer meant that the peat was already saturated and the rivers were full. A torrent of water poured into the narrow, steep-sided valleys of the East and West Lyn Rivers. Debris such as boulders and trees were swept along with the water and on the East Lyn collected to form a dam. Water built up behind this dam until it burst causing a solid wall of water nearly 15 metres high to rush down the valley. This wall of water moved huge rocks and boulders, some weighing 16 tonnes.

The holiday town of Lynmouth was located at the confluence of the East and West Lyn Rivers. As the water moved through the town many buildings were destroyed and 34 people died. The flood caused huge financial loss as well as great cost to human life and the local community.

After the disaster attempts were made to ensure that this would not occur again. The course of the East Lyn River was widened and the banks strengthened. An overflow area was built and the West Lyn River was rechannelled. Bridges were rebuilt with higher arches whilst houses and hotels were built further away from the river. The Environment Agency today ensures that the rivers are kept clear of debris.

Wildlife in Exmoor

Exmoor provides habitats for many different animals and plants (**H**).

H Wildlife habitats

With the variety of habitats Exmoor supports a large number of plant and animal species.

Coastland
Cliffs provide nesting sites for the guillemot, razorbill and even peregrine falcon. A salt marsh is found at Porlock and contains animals and plants which have adapted to the conditions. It provides a feeding ground for the curlew.

Woodland
Ancient woodland up to 400 years old supports much wildlife due to the variety of trees and other types of vegetation. Red, fallow and roe deer live in the woods.

Rivers and streams
These water courses and their banks offer a **wetland** habitat for many small mammals and insects. Many rivers have brown trout and are the spawning ground for salmon.

Moorland
Wet and acidic soils allow grasses and sedges to grow. Some animals like the red deer roam freely over most of the land whilst the Exmoor ponies are enclosed.

Heathland
Free draining soils allow heather, bracken and gorse to grow. Heathland is burnt to provide fresh grazing land and prevent shrubs and trees from becoming established.

Farmland and villages
Fields are separated by hedgerows. The older the hedgerow the wider the variety of shrubs. Hedgerows provide habitats for many animals. Farm buildings may have bats or owls living in them.

5 Exmoor National Park

Settlement patterns

Settlement patterns are influenced by the nature of the landscape. The poor soil, harsh climate and exposed areas on the moorlands discourage people from living there (see **E** and **G** on pages 86 and 87). The small towns of Porlock, Dulverton and Lynton act as centres of employment and services for the surrounding rural areas. The smaller villages, hamlets and farmsteads are found throughout the area up to a height of about 365 metres.

Many of the small villages used to have a number of services such as a shop, post office and school. As with many rural areas in the UK a decrease in job opportunities has meant that young people move away to seek work elsewhere. This is known as rural depopulation. Often older, retired people move into rural areas resulting in an ageing population. Services such as schools are no longer required. People now shop in supermarkets where there is more choice and only use their local shop occasionally. Many village shops have been forced to close although some survive due to tourism. Exmoor has also experienced the growth of **second homes** which can further contribute to the decline of rural services.

Dunster – a honeypot

Dunster is a **honeypot** town located at the junction of the A396 and the A39 on the eastern edge of Exmoor (see **G** on page 87). It has many attractions such as the nearby beach and steam railway as well as historic buildings (**I**). Dunster Castle, now owned by the National Trust, hosts many events throughout the year and is open to the public. The town has narrow streets of mediaeval homes which were occupied by the woollen workers. Tudor and Georgian buildings can be seen as well as a seventeenth-century working water-mill. The town's narrow streets lead to a bottleneck in the peak season.

Activities

Consider the different strategies below for reducing visitor pressure in Dunster. Discuss the pros and cons of each and decide which should be adopted. Explain your decision.

- Do not give planning permission for the development of new accommodation for visitors.
- Encourage people to visit Dunster at times of the year when visitor pressure is less.
- Try to promote other areas in Exmoor, so reducing pressure on Dunster.
- Remove road signs which attract people to Dunster.
- Increase the charges for car parking.
- Do nothing and hope that the pressure will eventually put people off.

I Main street in Dunster

Themes and Issues: National Parks in the UK

	1971	1981	1991
Agriculture/forestry/fisheries	25.0	23.5	21.2
Manufacturing	7.2	8.0	5.0
Construction	6.4	7.0	6.4
Energy/water/transport	4.4	5.0	4.5
Service industries (including tourism)	57.0	56.5	62.9

J Employment data for Exmoor (% employed in each industry)
(Source: Exmoor Census Data)

Activities

1. Use the information in table **J** to draw a graph(s) to show changes in employment.
2. Describe the changes in employment and try to explain why these have taken place.

Employment in Exmoor

Exmoor provides a range of job opportunities with most people working in agriculture, forestry and tourism (**J**). Over the last 20 years there has been a decline in Exmoor's more traditional occupations such as agriculture. More and more people are looking for jobs outside the National Park or are providing services for visitors.

Farming in Exmoor

The harsh conditions in much of Exmoor mean that sheep farming is the main farming land use. The sheep need to be hardy to withstand the conditions. Sheep have grazed the area for over 3000 years. Sheep eat the heather, grasses and seedlings and so help produce the scenery of Exmoor (see **G** on page 87). As with many other National Parks diversification is encouraged. There are a few dairy farms on the boundary of the park where the climate is less severe. Porlock Vale and Brendon Hills provide grade 1 and 2 (very good) arable land. High yields of cereals, linseed and potatoes are grown.

Farming changes and the environment

Improved technology has increased production. The use of fertilisers and chemicals to control pests and disease has become common. Sheep farmers also use selective breeding to produce the most suitable animals. These improvements and the encouragement given in subsidies by the European Union's (EU) Common Agricultural Policy led to overproduction. EU quotas were introduced to specify how much farmers can produce.

There is much pressure on the farmer to look after the environment. In 1993 Exmoor was designated an **Environmentally Sensitive Area** with the aim of maintaining the traditional Exmoor landscape. Farmers are able to receive payments for environmental management and grants for conservation work, such as hedgerow planting.

Much open moorland was ploughed up and enclosed, losing valuable habitat. The **National Park Authority** arranged management agreements which compensated farmers for not ploughing up the moorland. It also recognises the knowledge and experience of the local farmers and tries to support their activities. A Farm Liaison Officer is responsible for organising the Farm Conservation Scheme and for advising farmers on the many grants available.

Exmoor Producers

This project, formed in 1995, is financed by the EU, National Park Authority and Rural Development Commission. The aim is to produce a wide range of items which complement the Exmoor landscape, for example hazel chairs, furniture crafted from English hardwood, pottery and food such as flour, blue cheese and honey. Such a project could create valuable job opportunities in the rural areas.

5 Exmoor National Park

Leisure and recreation

Each year a million people visit Exmoor, mainly from the South East, the Midlands and South West. The majority arrive by car to admire the beautiful scenery whilst a small number take part in open air activities (**K**). Eighty per cent of visitors stay for the traditional week's or fortnight's holiday unlike many other National Parks. Short breaks are becoming more popular.

The role of the National Park Authority is to conserve the landscape whilst helping visitors to enjoy and appreciate the countryside. Care for the local community is vital so a balance between the various pressures must be struck. The priority of the National Park Authority is the protection of the landscape so it does not set out to develop tourism. However, tourism is recognised as being important to these rural communities so the National Park will promote aspects of tourism which do not damage the countryside.

K Activities people pursue in Exmoor

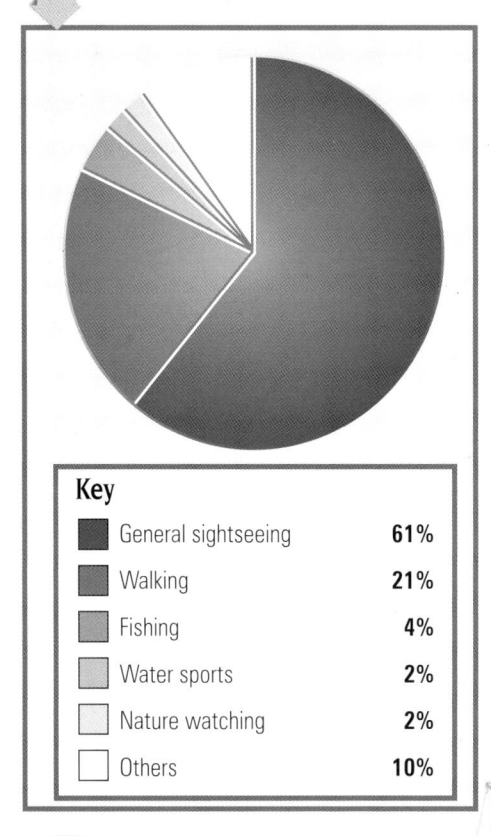

Key	
General sightseeing	61%
Walking	21%
Fishing	4%
Water sports	2%
Nature watching	2%
Others	10%

L Porlock weir

Exam practice

1. Study maps **D** and **E** on page 86.
   a. Make a list of the features that you might find in Exmoor National Park.
   b. Explain why there is a bay at Porlock. *(4 marks)*

2. Use maps **E** and **G** to describe the settlement pattern in Exmoor. Refer to relief, climate and accessibility in your answer. *(4 marks)*

3. Describe how the environment of Exmoor has been affected by farming. *(5 marks)*

4. What is the role of the National Park Authority. *(4 marks)*

5. Describe the effect the National Park Authority has had on the landscape of Exmoor. *(8 marks)*

6 PLANNING AND DEVELOPMENT OF THE NATIONAL PARKS

National Parks are working landscapes in which people have lived for centuries. They are areas of outstanding scenery which have been shaped by both natural and human forces. National Parks have received special protection so they can remain unspoilt and provide a great deal of enjoyment for people. Whilst there are conflicting demands on the landscape, each person has a right to use the countryside (**A**).

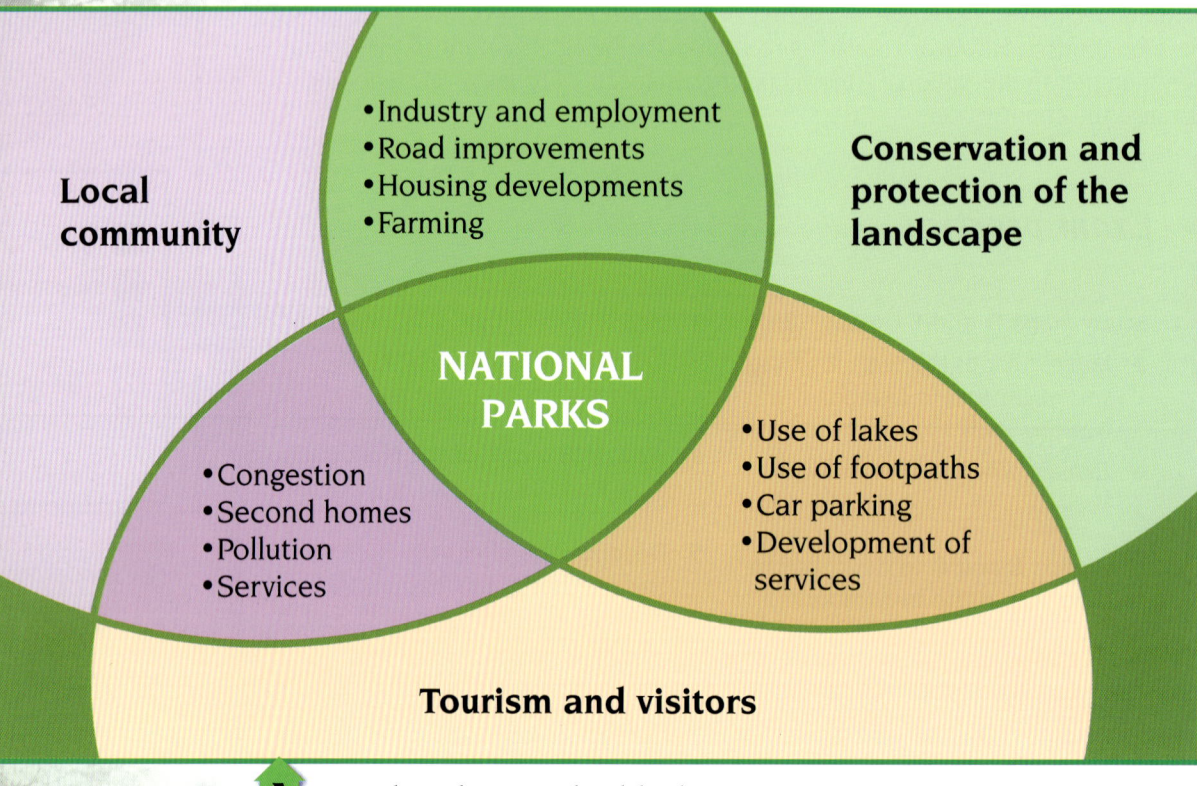

Local community

- Industry and employment
- Road improvements
- Housing developments
- Farming

Conservation and protection of the landscape

NATIONAL PARKS

- Congestion
- Second homes
- Pollution
- Services

- Use of lakes
- Use of footpaths
- Car parking
- Development of services

Tourism and visitors

A Demands on the National Park landscape

The Environment Act, 1995

For a number of years the environment has been high on the political agenda. There has been continuing debate about National Parks. In the Environment Act of 1995 the government:

- established independent **National Park Authorities** to run the parks;
- changed the purpose of National Parks to:
  – conserving and enhancing the natural beauty, wildlife and cultural heritage of the areas;
  – promoting opportunities for the understanding and enjoyment of the special qualities of the areas by the public.

In all cases, if conflict arises between the two purposes the first should take priority.

6 Planning and Development of the National Parks

The Act also indicated that:
- the National Park Authority had a duty to promote the social and economic well-being of local communities;
- membership of the National Park Authority should change so that there was greater local representation;
- any work carried out in the parks should have total regard for the two purposes.

Tourism still remains the greatest threat to the character of National Parks. A number of organisations have put together some general principles for tourism which would help keep the character of National Parks:

- Conservation – tourism could help protect the landscape by supporting conservation schemes. This could also be used to inform people about the possible damage tourists cause.
- Enjoyment – the opportunities for public open air recreation should be drawn from the special character of the different National Parks.
- Rural economy – tourism should encourage and support the local economy of the parks as it forms such an important part of the social and economic well-being of residents.
- Development – facilities for tourists should be sympathetic to the surrounding environment by recognising the special qualities of the landscape.
- Design – developments should enhance the landscape where possible, so careful siting, planning and design are essential.
- Marketing – tourism must inform people so they have a greater awareness and understanding of the countryside. In this way they might enjoy and appreciate the National Parks more fully.

The future

There are a number of areas within Britain which would benefit from more protection. The National Park debate continues in Scotland, particularly about Loch Lomond and the Cairngorms. Other successful measures have been taken to protect areas both within and outside the existing National Parks. These provide more local control over the use of the landscape, such as by the creation of **Sites of Special Scientific Interest** or Nature Reserves.

The demand for a wider range of outdoor activities and variety of facilities will continue to grow as people have greater mobility, more money and more leisure time, but the environmental impact is difficult to measure. The pressure of tourism can be seen vividly, for example in places where footpath erosion or traffic congestion have an impact on the surrounding environment.

National Parks must be wisely used so that people can enjoy the landscape in different ways without causing conflicts. The characteristics that have made these areas so special will continue to bring pleasure to those who live and work in them as well as to those who visit them.

Glossary

Access Agreement	an agreement with a landlord to allow people to walk on the land
Area of Outstanding Natural Beauty	a protected area for conservation, such as a coastline of particular value
bedding plane	the dividing line between two layers of sedimentary rock
braiding	when a river splits into two or more channels and then rejoins further downstream
brown earth soil	a soil that is rich in nutrients and supports forest vegetation
cavern	a hollow within limestone caused by water dissolving the rock
combe	a hollow found on a steep slope in a hillside
commercial farming	where crops or animals are grown or reared for sale
commute	to travel a long distance each day from the place of residence to the place of work
Countryside Commission	the official advisory body on National Parks and other protected areas
diversify (farming)	where farms engage in activities other than just farming to earn an extra income
Duchy of Cornwall	land owned by the Prince of Wales
Environmentally Sensitive Area	a scheme to help protect areas in the landscape from the effects of farming
eutrophication	water which experiences rapid plant growth leading to the loss of animals due to a lack of oxygen
extensive farming	farming which produces a low yield per hectare and therefore has to cover a wide area
fell rights	where a farmer is allowed to graze sheep on the fells by permission of the landowner
finite resource	a resource which will eventually run out
fission (nuclear)	the splitting of atoms to produce energy
fossil fuel	a fuel composed of the remains of dead plants and animals formed millions of years ago
glaciation	when sub-zero temperatures continue for a number of years causing ice to form and cover large areas of the earth
gley soil	a soil that occurs in wet areas with poor drainage
groyne	a barrier built out into the sea to slow down the movement of material
Heritage Area	an area of historical importance which has received protection

Glossary

honeypot	a tourist spot which attracts a large number of visitors each year
joint	a vertical crack in a rock
lateral erosion	sideways erosion of a river; occurs on the outside of a meander
levée	a natural or human built embankment along the side of a river
longshore drift	the movement of material along the coast as a result of the wave direction
misfit river	a river occupying a valley that it did not create
moorland	bleak open land covered in heather, bracken and coarse grasses
National Grid	the electricity transmission network which covers the UK
National Park Authority	a body that controls activities and planning within the National Parks
negative planning technique	used in popular areas, designed not to attract tourism by leaving roads windy and not providing facilities for visitors
North Atlantic Drift	a warm ocean current which flows across the Atlantic from tropical areas
park and ride scheme	a scheme which encourages people to park away from a popular area and use public transport for the final part of the journey
peat	a soil that is made up of decaying and dead vegetation
renewable energy	a form of energy that will not run out, such as wind and water
rock flour	when abrasion occurs at the bottom of a glacier, rocks are ground down to produce a flour
second home	a second house, only used at weekends or for holidays, owned by people who live somewhere else
Site of Special Scientific Interest	area of special environmental interest because of its plant and animal life
spring tide	when there is a large variation between the high and low tides
spur	land which protrudes out into an area of lower ground
storm surge	strong winds cause the level of the sea to rise more than expected
truncated spur	spurs that have been eroded away by ice moving along a valley
vertical erosion	the erosion of a river downwards into its bed
wetland	an area providing a wet environment which supports a range of animals and water plants

Index

Abermawr beach	18
abrasion	10, 11, 13, 17, 24
accessibility – footpaths	7, 25, 82–3
– roads	26, 44–5, 46, 47
agriculture (see farming)	
Areas of Outstanding Natural Beauty	32
arête	10, 12
bank erosion	25, 29
Bowness-on-Windermere	80–81
Brecon Beacons National Park	9, 82–3
Broads, the	6, 28–9
bypass	46–51
camping barns	56–7
car ownership	44, 76
Castlemartin peninsula	17
Castleton	38–43
caves/caverns	8, 9, 21–2, 40
climbing	13, 21, 23
coasts	8, 9, 16–19, 28, 88
commuting	39
congestion	23, 42, 45, 47, 80–81, 92
corrie	10–12, 14
Countryside Commission	6, 31
Cwm Idwal	10–13
dam	26–7, 72
Dartmoor National Park	8, 46–51
deposition	11, 13, 16, 18–19, 21, 25
diversification	55–7, 90
Dunster	89
employment	38, 42, 77, 90
Environment Act, 1995	6, 92
Environmentally Sensitive Areas	28–9, 55, 90
erosion	10–11, 19, 24–5, 29, 88
Exmoor National Park	9, 85–9
farming	7, 25, 27, 29, 52–7, 90
flood defence	28, 29
flooding	28, 88
footpath erosion	42, 82–4, 93
Forest Enterprise	27, 34–5
Forestry Commission	31, 34–5
forests (see woodland)	
fossil fuels	70
freeze-thaw	10, 11, 12, 22
glaciation	8, 10–15, 21, 82
Great Langdale	14–15
Gordale Scar	20–21
hanging valley	14–15
Haverigg wind farm	73
heathland	88
Heritage Area	30–31, 45, 85
highways strategy	32, 45
Home Farm	52–5
honeypot	20, 38–43, 46, 76–7, 80–1, 89
hydraulic action	17
hydroelectric power	72–3
ice (see glaciation)	
industry	39, 58–63, 64–9, 90, 92
Janet's Foss	20, 21
Lake District National Park	7, 8, 14, 15, 44, 52–5, 76–81
Land – ownership	6
– use	6, 35, 48, 54–5, 77, 87
limestone	20–23, 58–63
Loch Lomond Regional park	6, 34–5, 93
Lynmouth	88
Maentwrog	72–3
Malham	20–23
meander	25
Milford Haven	18, 64–9
moorland	8, 9, 88
moraine	11, 13–15, 21
motorways	44
Nant Ffrancon	10, 12–13
National Parks and Access to the Countryside Act	6
National Park Commission	6
National Park Authority	6, 45, 61, 73, 85, 90, 92, 93
New Forest Heritage Area	30–33, 45
Northumberland National Park	9, 24, 25
North York Moors National Park	9, 37
nuclear power	70–71
oil pollution	66–9
oil refining	64–6
Okehampton	46–9
park and ride	23, 27, 78
Peak National Park	6, 8, 26–7, 38–43, 44
Pembrokeshire Coast National Park	8, 16–19, 64–9
Pennine Way	8, 9
planning procedure	61
plantation (see woodland)	
plucking	10, 11, 13
pollution	29, 45, 66–8, 92
quarrying	58–63
rambling/walking	27
renewable energy	70, 72–5
reservoirs (Derwent, Howden, Ladybower)	26–7
ribbon lake	13, 14
River Breamish	24–5
roche moutonnée	12, 13
Rowardennan	34–5
Runnage Farm	56–7
sand dunes	19
satellite photographs	8–9, 33, 69
second homes	7, 80–81, 89, 92
Sea Empress	67–8
setting up of National Parks	6
settlement	20, 36–7, 38–43, 80–81, 85, 89, 92
Severn-Trent Water	26, 27
Site of Special Scientific Interest	27, 32, 34–5, 72, 78, 93
Snowdonia National Park	8, 10–14, 70–73
striations	13
Swinden Quarry	59–61
tarn	11, 12, 14–15, 20, 21
Texaco	64–9
tourism	7, 13, 19, 20, 23, 25, 27, 29, 32, 38–43, 46, 76–84, 91, 92–3
Trawsfynydd	70–71
truncated spurs	12
Upper Derwent valley	26–7
u-shaped valley	12–15
waterfalls	13, 21, 24
water treatment	27
Watlowes dry valley	20, 22
weathering	10, 11, 20, 22
wetland	32, 88
wildlife habitats	27, 88
Windermere	78, 80–81
wind power	73–5
woodland	27, 30–35, 88
Yorkshire Dales National Park	9, 20–23, 44, 58–61